COURAGEOUS
LEADERSHIP

BILL HYBELS

COURAGEOUS LEADERSHIP

ZONDERVAN™

GRAND RAPIDS, MICHIGAN 49530 USA

ZONDERVAN™

Courageous Leadership
Copyright © 2002 by Bill Hybels

International Trade Paper Edition

Requests for information should be addressed to:

Zondervan, *Grand Rapids, Michigan 49530*

ISBN 0-310-24881-7

Interior design by Nancy Wilson

Printed in the United States of America

03 04 05 06 07 08 /❖ DC/ 10 9 8

To Jon Rasmussen,
builder of buildings for God,
the best husband and father I have ever known,
and the best friend a man could ever have

Contents

Acknowledgments

As ANY TRUE LEADER WOULD EXPECT, IT TOOK A TEAM TO TURN THE idea of this book into reality. Valerie Bell did all the heavy lifting in the early days of this challenge. Not only did she pore over hundreds of pages of handwritten sermon notes, but she also listened with a writer's ear to new leadership talks I tried out in various settings. She deserves the credit for giving shape to the content of this material. My wife, Lynne, the best editor I have ever known, agreed to do the final edit of the manuscript in exchange for household improvements we should have made long ago. The deal was a no-brainer.

My assistant, Jean, always winds up playing a major part in everything I do, and this project was no exception. Jim and Chris Holden provided us with a place to write when it looked like the deadline was going to push our family over the edge. Jim Mellado kept his arm around me, reminding me that this book would really help church leaders.

And what can I say about the congregation who has allowed me to stumble and bumble my way toward some degree of leadership maturity? I owe Willow Creek Community Church a debt I will never be able to pay. It lives out the Acts 2 dream better than any church I have ever seen anywhere in the world. To have been its pastor for twenty-seven years has been an honor for which I have thanked God every single day.

Introduction

I'VE WAITED THIRTY YEARS TO WRITE THIS BOOK. DURING THOSE YEARS I authored many books, but none that I felt as strongly about as this one. The words and ideas that fill the pages to follow are not abstract concepts to me; they represent the activity and passion of my life.

I have presented some of the material in this book in conferences and workshops. Throughout the years I was tempted to gather those talks together in book form, but in the end I always concluded that I wasn't quite ready to make a contribution to the wider Christian community about the importance of the spiritual gift of leadership. Every time I thought I might be ready to start writing, I faced a challenge at Willow Creek Community Church that showed me I wasn't. And time and again I sensed the confirmation of the Holy Spirit: "Be patient, Bill."

The reason this book needed to be "on pause" for so long was that I needed to become seasoned enough to write it. In the early years of my ministry my boldness and decisiveness were not matched by equal measures of wisdom and sensitivity, so I quickly compiled a list of leadership mistakes worthy of a page in Guinness. But by God's grace, I was surrounded by some loving people who were willing to continue the adventure with me while I learned. Together, we have matured through a process that has spanned almost three decades.

Some months ago I celebrated my fiftieth birthday, an event that prompted more reflection than I had anticipated. As a result of examining both my past and present experiences as a leader, I concluded that my thirty-year graduate class on leadership—fleshed out in the real-life laboratory of a local church—had finally prepared me to write about the strategic importance of the spiritual gift of leadership. I don't mean to imply that I've "graduated." I will always be a student, will always be striving to grow, when it comes to leadership. But I do sense the Holy Spirit telling me that it's time for me to share what I'm learning with other students. So in the following chapters, I've done my best to describe the function, instincts, and scope of what leaders must do. This is not a book on leadership theories, but rather on proven leadership practice.

If leaders in business, government, or education increase their competence through reading this book, that's fine. But I am not writing primarily to them. In the end, even though their work may be exceedingly important, the cause to which they have dedicated their leadership skills has one thing lacking: it does not have the power to change the world. What makes my heart beat fast is engaging with leaders in local churches, because I believe that the local church is the hope of the world. I believe to the core of my being that local church leaders have the potential to be the most influential force on planet earth. If they "get it," and get on with it, churches can become the redemptive centers that Jesus intended them to be. Dynamic teaching, creative worship, deep community, effective evangelism, and joyful service will combine to renew the hearts and minds of seekers and believers alike, strengthen families, transform communities, and *change the world*.

So that's my hope in writing this book—that men and women with the spiritual gift of leadership will begin to lead energetically, joyfully, and effectively in local churches everywhere, and that under the blessing of God and the leadership of these devoted servants of Christ the church will become what it is meant to be: a force against which the very gates of hell cannot prevail.

CHAPTER ONE

The Stakes of Leadership

TEN DAYS AFTER THE ATTACKS ON THE WORLD TRADE CENTER Towers, I stood in the rubble at Ground Zero, overwhelmed by the aftermath of one of the most horrific events in history.

On that world-changing morning of September 11, 2001, Manhattan, New York, became a war zone. The terrorists took no prisoners, held no hostages. Death was the only option they offered, so three thousand ordinary people died that day, most without an opportunity for a final embrace or even a last good-bye.

The New York City officials who invited me to tour Ground Zero led me past the check points and into "The Pit," the area immediately surrounding the fallen towers. In the grim shadows of the huge cranes that slowly shifted scraps of twisted metal, rescue workers dug through the rubble, and bucket brigades passed pails of debris from hand to hand. The workers moved silently, listening, I knew, for the sounds—any sounds—of survivors.

Those ninety minutes will stay with me for the rest of my life.

Words cannot convey, nor television screens capture, the enormity of the devastation I saw for that hour and a half. For the first thirty minutes the only two words I could utter were, "No way!" And I said them over and over again.

In my imagination I had envisioned the two slender towers sinking into a pile of debris that would fit easily within the confines of a large football stadium. My mental picture was big—and tragic—enough, but reality was a hundred times more tragic. A square mile of ruin. Numerous city blocks obliterated. One of the *smaller* buildings that came down was over forty stories high. Several larger buildings, still standing when I was there, were buckling and would have to be demolished. Some looked like the Oklahoma Federal Building with its front blown off. Others, blocks away, had windows shattered. The sheer enormity of what happened that day took my breath away.

I said "No way!" again when I saw the dedication of the rescue workers, many of whom were still digging after ten days, with bloodied hands and blistered feet, because their firefighting buddies were buried under the piles of twisted steel. How can I describe what it was like to be with them, to look into their eyes and see the profound coupling of utter exhaustion and unyielding determination? There were hundreds and hundreds of them. I found myself torn between wanting to grab hold of them and say, "Please stop. You've got to rest. You've got to go home," and at the same time wanting to pat them on the back and say, "Don't give up! If I were under that pile of destruction I'd want someone like you digging for me."

I've never been in war, so I've never seen men and women like that. I've never seen people who were nearly dead on their feet walk back into the carnage because they couldn't do otherwise. I'll never forget it. People like that ennoble the human spirit. They remind us that we can still be heroic.

Later in the day, I was driven by cab to a designated place several blocks away from the rescue effort, where family and friends were posting pictures of loved ones on a crudely constructed bulletin board that ran for hundreds of feet along the sidewalk. As I looked at the photographs crammed from top to bottom, side to side, again I said, "No way!" No way should men, women, and children have to live with this kind of loss and grief.

Back and forth walked the people left behind. For twenty-four hours every day they wandered like zombies along the city streets, hoping against hope that *someone* could tell them *something* about their father, their daughter, their friend. There was no way they could move on with their lives. They couldn't eat or sleep. They couldn't go home without *some* information, *some* piece of news, *some* degree of closure.

I could understand their tenacity. What else could they do? If my family—Lynne or Shauna or Todd—or my friends were among those missing beneath the rubble, I would do the same. I'd plaster their pictures all over that wall; I'd grab people by the collar if I thought they could offer me one little shred of information or hope.

As I hailed a cab to take me back to my hotel, I felt like screaming my next "No way!" in an attempt to block out the bitterest truth of all, that all this suffering, this holocaust, was caused not by a natural calamity or even some freak accident, but by the deliberate schemes of fellow human beings. No earthquake, no shift in geological plates caused this wreckage. No flood, tornado, or hurricane did this. The death and destruction surrounding me were the direct result of the careful plans of people so caught up in radical political beliefs and so filled with hatred that as they watched the television coverage of Ground Zero they high-fived each other and jumped for joy.

"No way!" I cried again. *There's no way evil can run this deep.* But it did. No matter how incomprehensible was the scene surrounding me, the enormity of evil behind it could not be denied.

But strangely, while the ashes smoldered around me and grief overwhelmed me, even then, a profound hope rose in my heart. Slicing through the anguished "no ways" reverberating in my mind were the words I had repeated ten thousand times before, but now they cut with the flash of urgency. *The local church is the hope of the world. The local church is the hope of the world.* I could see it so clearly.

I do not intend to minimize the contribution of the many fine organizations performing wonderful, loving, charitable acts in the middle of the misery of Ground Zero. The Red Cross was handing out work gloves and breathing masks, fresh socks and clean boots. Restaurants were setting up barbecue grills on sidewalks and cooking free food for rescue workers. Soft drink manufacturers donated beverages. Humanitarian groups and corporations set up trust funds with hundreds of millions of dollars for the families of victims. Money poured in. For all these actions Americans should be proud. And I certainly am.

But work of a deeper kind was happening behind the scenes in downtown Manhattan during those days. While many pastors and church volunteers joined with charitable agencies in helping to meet physical and material needs, they also went beyond that—far beyond it. Ordinary Christ-followers like you and me sat in restaurants, office buildings, and temporary shelters, addressing with courage and sensitivity the deep concerns of the *soul*. Meeting one-on-one and in small groups, they cried with people. They prayed with people. They listened. They embraced. They soothed.

It happened twenty-four hours a day for days on end. It was the untold media story, the clip that never made it to the network news. While many fine organizations met the external needs of people, the church was there to do what it is uniquely equipped to do: to offer healing to deeply wounded souls.

That experience had and still has a powerful impact on me. It underscored, yet again, the convictions that have been growing in me for the past thirty years—that the church has an utterly unique mission to fulfill on planet Earth, and that the future of our society depends, largely, on whether or not church leaders understand that mission and mobilize their congregations accordingly. Hopefully, the events of September 11, 2001, will never be repeated. But there will be other tragedies, other acts of violence, other losses that grieve our hearts and break the heart of God. Will the Church of Jesus Christ be a light bright enough to shine in such darkness?

But wait. I'm running ahead of myself. Let me rewind the videotape and start at the beginning of my experience with the church.

THE BEAUTY OF THE CHURCH

IN THE EARLY SEVENTIES I had an experience so powerful that it divided my life into before and after. I was a college student taking a required course in New Testament Studies to complete my major. To my way of thinking this class was guaranteed to be brain-numbingly boring. A required Bible class? It had "flat liner" written all over it. I was sure that the only challenge this class would offer me would be the challenge of trying to stay awake.

As I staked out my usual claim to a back row seat and assumed a comfortable slouch—legs extended, arms folded—I had no idea that a spiritual ambush awaited me. Toward the end of the lecture, just when I thought it was time to pack it up and leave, the professor, Dr. Gilbert Bilezikian, decided he wasn't quite finished for the day. Closing his notes, he stepped out from behind the lectern. Then he bared his soul to a room full of unsuspecting twenty-year-olds.

"Students," he said, "there was once a community of believers who were so totally devoted to God that their life together was charged with the Spirit's power.

"In that band of Christ-followers, believers loved each other with a radical kind of love. They took off their masks and shared their lives with one another. They laughed and cried and prayed and sang and served together in authentic Christian fellowship.

"Those who had more shared freely with those who had less until socioeconomic barriers melted away. People related together in ways that bridged gender and racial chasms, and celebrated cultural differences.

"Acts 2 tells us that this community of believers, this church, offered unbelievers a vision of life that was so beautiful it took their breath away. It was so bold, so creative, so dynamic that they couldn't resist it. Verse 47 tells us that 'the Lord added to their number daily those who were being saved.'"

Dr. Bilezikian's unscripted words were as much a lament as they were a dream, a sad longing for the restoration of the first century church. I had never imagined a more compelling vision. In fact, that day I didn't just see the vision; I was seized by it.

Suddenly, there were tears in my eyes and a responsive chord rising up in my soul.

Where, I wondered, *had that beauty gone?*

Why was that power not evident in the contemporary church?

Would the Christian community ever see that potential realized again?

Since that day, I have been held hostage to the powerful picture of the Acts 2 dream painted in that college classroom. In the weeks and months after that first lecture, I was haunted by questions. *What if a true community of God could be established in the twentieth century? What if what happened in Jerusalem could happen in Chicago?* Such a movement of God would transform this world and usher people into the next.

I was a goner, utterly captured by a single vision of the potential beauty of the local church. In 1975 that vision led me and a handful of colleagues to start Willow Creek Community Church. Now, almost thirty years later, that vision still rivets my attention, sparks my passion, and calls forth the best effort I can give.

THE POWER OF THE CHURCH

ONE MAJOR FACET OF the beauty of the local church is its power to transform the human heart. I remember exactly where I was when I saw clearly the world's need for this transforming power. You could say I was "provoked" to this understanding.

It was the mid-eighties. I'd been out of the country for weeks on a speaking trip and was returning to the U.S. via San Juan, Puerto Rico. Having been outside CNN range for most of the trip, I was eager to reconnect with the world and discover what had happened while I was gone. So I bought a *USA Today,* positioned my Styrofoam coffee cup in the "no-spill" zone under my seat in the gate area, unfolded the paper, and hungrily ate up the news.

Then the commotion began. Two young boys (brothers I assumed) started squabbling with each other. The older kid appeared to be seven or eight, the younger one around five. I watched them for a few seconds over the top of my paper, mildly irritated by the disturbance they were causing. But compared to the information of worldwide importance I was busy digesting, a childish tussle between brothers was hardly worth attending to. *Boys will be boys,* I thought, and resumed my reading.

Then, *whack!* I lowered my newspaper. It was obvious that the older boy had just slapped the younger one squarely across the face. The small boy was crying, a nasty welt already rising on his cheek.

I nervously scanned the crowd, looking for the adult who was responsible for these kids, the adult who could stop this violence.

Then the entire gate area was silenced by a sound that none of us will forget for a long, long time. It was the sound of a closed fist smashing into a face. While the little boy was still crying from the first slap, the older boy had wound up and belted him again, literally knocking the little guy off his feet.

That was more than I could take. "Where are these kids' parents?" I blurted into the crowded gate area. No response.

As I raced toward the boys, the bully grabbed the little guy by the hair and started pounding his face into the tile floor.

Bam! Bam! Bam!

I heard the final boarding announcement for my flight, but I was too sickened by this violence to abandon my mission. I grabbed the older boy by the arm and hauled him off the younger one, then held them as far apart as I could. With one arm extending out to a kid with a bloody face and the other straining to stop a boy with murder in his eyes, I knew I was holding a human tragedy in my hands.

Just then the ticket agent came up to me and said, "If you're Mr. Hybels, you've got to board this plane immediately. It's leaving now!"

Reluctantly, I loosened my hold on the boys, gathered my things, and rushed backwards down the gangplank, shouting a plea to the ticket agent, "Keep those kids apart! Please! And find their parents!"

I stumbled onto the plane and managed to find my seat, but I was badly shaken by what had just happened. I couldn't get the sights and sounds of the violence I had witnessed out of my mind. I grabbed a sports magazine and tried to read an article but I couldn't concentrate. I looked in the entertainment magazine to see what movie would be shown and hoped it would be something captivating enough to distract me.

But while I waited, I sensed the Holy Spirit telling me not to try to purge my mind so quickly. *Think about what you saw. Consider the implications. Let your heart be gripped by this reality.*

As I consciously chose to dwell on what I had seen, I was flooded with thoughts about the older kid's life. I wondered where his parents were. I wondered what kind of experience he was having in school. I wondered if there was anybody in his life offering him love and guidance and hope. I wondered what his future held. If he's throwing fists at the age of eight, what will he be throwing at eighteen? Knives? Bullets? Where will he end up? In a nice house with a good wife and a satisfying job? Or in a jail cell? In an early grave?

Then I was prompted by the Spirit to consider what might change the trajectory of this kid's life. I scrolled through the options. *Maybe,* I thought, *if we elect some really great government officials who will pass new legislation, maybe that will help a kid like this.*

But will it? Don't misunderstand me. I know that what governments do is very important. Writing legislation for the good of society is a noble, worthy task. Public service is an honorable vocation. But politicians, no matter how sincere their motivation, can only do so much.

For eight years during the decade of the nineties I went to Washington, D.C., every month to meet in the foremost centers of power with some of the highest elected officials in our country. What I discovered was not how powerful those people are, but how limited their power really is. All they can actually do is rearrange the yard markers on the playing field of life. They can't change a human heart. They can't heal a wounded soul. They can't turn hatred into love. They can't bring about repentance, forgiveness, reconciliation, peace. They can't get to the core problem of the kid I saw in the airport and millions of others like him.

I scrolled through every other option I could think of, considering what they have to offer. Businessmen can provide sorely needed jobs. Wise educators can teach useful knowledge of the world. Self-help programs can offer effective methods of behavior modification. Advanced psychological techniques can aid self-understanding. And all of this is good. But can any of it truly transform the human heart?

I believe that only one power exists on this sorry planet that can do that. It's the power of the love of Jesus Christ, the love that conquers sin and wipes out shame and heals wounds and reconciles enemies and patches broken dreams and ultimately changes the world, one life at a time. And what grips my heart every day is the knowledge that the radical message of that transforming love has been given to the church.

That means that in a very real way the future of the world rests in the hands of local congregations like yours and mine. It's the church or it's lights out. Without churches so filled with the power of God that they can't help but spill goodness and peace and love and joy into the world, depravity will win the day; evil will flood the world. But it doesn't have to be that way. Strong, growing communities of faith can turn the tide of history. They can!

Don't bother looking elsewhere. The church is it.

THE POTENTIAL OF THE CHURCH

THAT GRUESOME SCENE IN the San Juan airport was a graphic illustration of the problems that beset our world. The Holy Spirit's prompting as I sat on the plane reminded me that the transforming power of God is the answer to that problem. Some time after that trip, I was given a real-life picture of the incredible potential of that transforming power.

I had just finished presenting my weekend message at Willow and I was standing in the bullpen, talking to people. A young married couple approached me, placed a blanketed bundle in my arms, and asked me to pray for their baby.

As I asked what the baby's name was, the mother pulled back the blanket that had covered the infant's face. I felt my knees begin to buckle. I thought I was going to faint. Had the father not steadied me I may well have keeled over. In my arms was the most horribly deformed baby I had ever seen. The whole center of her tiny face was caved in. How she kept breathing I will never know.

All I could say was, "Oh my . . . oh my . . . oh my."

"Her name is Emily," said the mother. "We've been told she has about six weeks to live," added the father. "We would like you to pray that before she dies she will know and feel our love."

Barely able to mouth the words, I whispered, "Let's pray." Together we prayed for Emily. Oh, did we pray. As I handed her back to her parents I asked, "Is there anything we can do for you, any way that we as a church can serve you during this time?"

The father responded with words that still amaze me. He said, "Bill, we're okay. Really we are. We've been in a loving small group for years. Our group members knew that this pregnancy had complications. They were at our house the night we learned the news, and they were at the hospital when Emily was delivered. They helped us absorb the reality of the whole thing. They even cleaned our house and fixed our meals when we brought her home. They pray for us constantly and call us several times every day. They are even helping us plan Emily's funeral."

Just then three other couples stepped forward and surrounded Emily and her parents. "We always attend church together as a group," said one of the group members.

It was a picture I will carry to my grave, a tight-knit huddle of loving brothers and sisters doing their best to soften one of the cruelest blows life can throw. After a group prayer, they all walked up the side aisle toward our lobby.

Where, I wondered as they left, *would that family be, where would they go, how would they handle this heartbreak, without the church?*

There is nothing like the local church when it's working right. Its beauty is indescribable. Its power is breathtaking. Its potential is unlimited. It comforts the grieving and heals the broken in the context of community. It builds bridges to seekers and offers truth to the confused. It provides resources for those in need and opens its arms to the forgotten, the downtrodden, the disillusioned. It breaks the chains of addictions, frees the oppressed, and offers belonging to the marginalized of this world. Whatever the capacity for human suffering, the church has a greater capacity for healing and wholeness.

Still to this day, the potential of the local church is almost more than I can grasp. No other organization on earth is like the church. Nothing even comes close.

THE VITALITY OF THE CHURCH

NOTHING COMES CLOSE . . . if the church is working right. But that's a big *if*. In the mid-eighties, when I began to travel more, I couldn't ignore the gap that existed between churches that were living out their purposes and flourishing—reaching seekers, growing up strong believers, putting their arms around the poor, lifting broken lives—and those that seemed to be on the verge of failure, going through empty motions that appeared to impact no one.

Flourishing or failing? Everywhere I went, I found myself asking, *What makes the difference? What is the key to the vitality of thriving churches?* I know that ultimately the beauty and power of the church flow from the mind of God and depend on the blessing of God. But on a more human level, what do prevailing churches have in common?

Is it location? Church growth experts claim that location is crucial, and in my head I agree with them, but time and again I have discovered thriving churches in the most unlikely places.

I've visited vital, growing churches in Northern Ireland, located in the middle of communities grievously touched by what locals call "the Troubles." I preached recently in a thriving church located in the heart of Soweto, the impoverished South African township that boiled over into revolution before the end of apartheid. On the other side of the spectrum, in places like Newport Beach, California, where everyone is so affluent you might think they never sense their need for God, I've seen churches packed with people whose hearts are aflame with devotion to Christ.

Affluent or ghetto, serene or war-torn, tropical or alpine, congested urban or sleepy rural, American or otherwise, location seems to impact the vitality of a church far less than most of us think.

Well then, I thought, maybe denomination is the determining factor. Maybe I can discover a particular denomination that has a corner on the market.

But my travels did not confirm that. I learned of a thousand-year-old Anglican church in the United Kingdom that baptizes scores of people every year, a Kansas City Episcopal church that recently purchased a hundred acres to accommodate its growth, and a Lutheran congregation in Phoenix that is using its resources to address the needs of the unemployed and senior citizens in remarkably creative and effective ways. Baptist, Methodist, Evangelical Free, Quaker, non-denoms, inter-denoms—it doesn't matter. Within every denomination, and beyond, I have discovered prevailing churches.

If not location or denomination, perhaps an ideal facility is the key to success. But no. Most certainly not. In barns and theaters, hotels and doublewide trailers—in every imaginable kind of inadequate facility—I have discovered wonderfully thriving churches.

Perhaps, I thought, I have overlooked an obvious factor. Maybe the key to thriving churches is great preaching. But I didn't have to look any further than the United States to debunk that theory. Although many preaching-centered churches attract large crowds, their impact on the community is often negligible. The church is packed for an hour on Sunday, but empty during the week. Sermon junkies tend to stay in their comfortable pews, growing ever more knowledgeable while becoming ever less involved in the surrounding community. Conversions are rare because there's little outreach. Community experience is shallow because there is no infrastructure of small groups. The body is being fed and satisfied in a corporate teaching setting, but that's about all that's happening.

I don't mean to minimize the importance of effective teaching and preaching; the church withers without them. But good teaching and preaching alone do not ensure ministry vitality.

There are probably other assumed keys to church vitality I could also debunk, but being the impatient person I am I want to leap to the punch line. So here it is: What flourishing churches have in common is that they are led by people who possess and deploy the spiritual gift of leadership. Whenever and wherever I have found a high-impact, Acts 2, prevailing church, I have also discovered a little band of brothers and sisters who were humbly and prayerfully providing the vision, the strategy, and the inspiration that enabled an entire congregation to bear fruit abundantly. Please understand, it's not that I believe the gift of leadership is more important than other gifts. It's simply that people with the gift of leadership are uniquely equipped to come up with strategies and structures that provide opportunities for other people to use their gifts most effectively. Leaders see the big picture and understand how to help others find their place of service within that picture.

Through the years I've met a wide array of leaders. Some were in their later years while others were surprisingly young. Some were college educated while many lacked formal training altogether. Some had seminary backgrounds while others came out of the marketplace. I know of a thriving church in Tijuana, Mexico, that is led by a doctor. In Rockford, Illinois, a stockbroker formed a team that gave birth to a church. A dentist in New Jersey did the same. The common thread connecting all these leaders was that they recognized and developed their leadership gifts, submitted them to God, and used them as effectively as they could. The result? Prevailing churches.

LEADERSHIP HISTORY 101

I SHOULDN'T HAVE BEEN surprised that behind the scenes of every prevailing ministry I discovered courageous, servant-oriented leaders. Throughout history, whenever God was ready to begin a new work, he would tap a potential leader on the shoulder and give him or her a leadership assignment. In the Old Testament, he chose leaders like Moses, David, Nehemiah, and Esther. In the

New Testament he chose people like Peter and Paul. In more recent times, when a wayward church community needed to be called back to its true heart and mission, God used leaders like Martin Luther, John Calvin, and John Wesley to be the initial catalysts for change.

Ten years ago I sat in a little restaurant during my summer study break and wrote these words: *The local church is the hope of the world and its future rests primarily in the hands of its leaders.* For the first time, I realized that from a human perspective the outcome of the redemptive drama being played out on planet Earth will be determined by how well church leaders lead. Many churches are filled with sincere, talented, godly people who would love to leverage their spiritual gifts in order to impact the world for Christ. The question is this: Will the men and women who have been entrusted with leadership gifts take their gifts seriously, develop them fully, and deploy them courageously, so that the willing and gifted believers in their churches can work together to make a difference in the world?

Romans 12:8 tells those of us who have the gift of leadership that we had better sit up and take notice, we had better "lead with diligence." Why? Because the Church, the bride of Christ, upon which the eternal destiny of the world depends, will flourish or falter largely on the basis of how we lead. If you're a leader, please reread that sentence and let it sink into your consciousness. Also, please understand that I am not writing about leadership simply to highlight this particular gift. My ultimate concern is not leadership. For me, the bottom line is the Acts 2 church. But I am absolutely convinced that the church will never reach her full redemptive potential until men and women with the leadership gift step up and lead.

People supernaturally gifted to lead must yield themselves fully to God. They must cast powerful, biblical, God-honoring visions. They must build effective, loving, clearly focused teams. They must fire up Christ followers to give their absolute best for God. And they must insist with pit bull determination that

> *the gospel be preached,*
> *the lost be found,*
> *the believers be equipped,*
> *the poor be served,*
> *the lonely be enfolded into community,*
> *and God gets the credit for it all.*

Scripture tells us exactly what will happen if leaders will do what God has called and gifted them to do. The forces of darkness will be pushed back. The Evil One, who has had his way in the world for far too long, will be forced to give ground. And the church will fulfill the redemptive purpose for which Christ called it into being.

I don't know about you, but when I think about the world we live in—a world where evil manifests itself in ways that defy imagination, where little boys in airports smash each other's faces, and where madmen reign terror on innocents—I can't help but commit myself with even greater fervor to the beautiful, powerful, vital Church of Jesus Christ. Where else would I want to employ the leadership gifts God has graciously given me? The church is the hope of the world!

CHAPTER TWO

A Leader's Most Potent Weapon

The Power of Vision

Y OU DON'T HAVE TO BE A CYNIC TO FEEL A LITTLE SKEPTICAL WHEN someone starts talking about changing the world. Even if you agree that the world is due for some major reconstruction, you probably consider the chances of such change to be slim. But when God fuels a dream, and a leader becomes inspired—well, who knows what might happen?

For instance, in 1774 a leader named John Adams boldly declared his vision of a new nation, a union of thirteen states independent from the parliament and the King of England. Against great odds, his words came true. Within two years of his prophetic proclamation, the United States of America was born.

In 1789 William Wilberforce stood before the British Parliament and eloquently cried out for the day when men, women, and children would no longer be bought and sold like farm animals. Each year for the next eighteen years his bill was defeated, but he continued his tireless campaign against slavery. Finally, in 1833, four days before his death, Parliament passed a bill completely abolishing slavery.

In the late 1800s, two brothers, Wilbur and Orville Wright, announced that "the age of the flying machine" had arrived. Ten years of disappointing experiments followed. But on December 17, 1903, the Wright brothers made history when their small biplane lifted off a sandy beach in Kitty Hawk, North Carolina. The age of air travel was born.

In the early twentieth century a dynamic industrialist named Henry Ford stood in front of his ragtag band of employees and vowed to make automobile transportation affordable for the average American family. The nation laughed out loud. But barely fifteen years later, millions of Ford's Model T automobiles had been bought and sold at a cost of just $290 each.

In the 1940s a young evangelist named Billy Graham had a radical dream. He and a few college buddies envisioned packed stadiums where people far from God could hear the proclamation of the gospel. As of this year, 210 million people have heard Billy Graham preach live, while over one billion have heard Dr. Graham present the gospel via television and radio.

And who can forget 1963? Dr. Martin Luther King Jr. stood on the steps of the Lincoln Memorial in Washington, D.C. and painted a picture of a world without prejudice, hatred, or racism. "I have a dream that my four children will one day live in a nation where they will not be judged by the color of their skin but by the content of their character." Although Dr. King was cruelly assassinated, his dream lives on. Almost forty years later his passion guides our nation as racial barriers fall. (Though not as quickly as most of us would like.)

Ten years later and closer to home, Dr. Gilbert Bilezikian stood in front of a college classroom and dreamed about building a prevailing church. "There was once a church . . ." Twenty-seven years later, the handful of us who started Willow Creek Community Church still bawl like babies when we remember the power of his words. It is no exaggeration to say that everything we're seeing today at Willow Creek and in the thousands of other churches in the Willow Creek Association (WCA) worldwide was inspired by his impassioned words.

Scroll through a list like that and even a skeptic has to see that inspired leaders actually can change their worlds. So don't bother questioning the possibility of world change. Ask, instead, a question far more pertinent: "What did all those leaders have in common?"

THE MOST POTENT WEAPON FOR WORLD CHANGE: VISION

WHAT THEY HAD IN common was a compelling vision. Vision is at the very core of leadership. Take vision away from a leader and you cut out his or her heart. Vision is the fuel that leaders run on. It's the energy that creates action. It's the fire that ignites the passion of followers. It's the clear call that sustains focused effort year after year, decade after decade, as people offer consistent and sacrificial service to God.

Proverbs 29:18 says, "Where there is no vision, the people are unrestrained." They can't focus, can't reach their goal, can't follow their dream. An older translation says, "Without vision, the people perish." I've seen it with my own eyes—without vision, people lose the vitality that makes them feel alive.

I'm not saying that the only thing churches need is visionary leadership. When a local church is discouraged or demoralized, it turns to its shepherds, its artists, and its mercy-gifted folks for a fresh wave of encouragement. When the church needs organization and order, it turns to gifted administrators and says, "Do something about this chaos." When it needs edification it turns to people with the gift of teaching.

But when a church needs a God-honoring, kingdom-advancing, heart-thumping vision, it turns to its leaders. That's because God put in the leader's arsenal the potent offensive weapon called vision. The goal of this chapter is to unravel the complexities of vision so that we leaders can learn to unleash its power in our churches. This is where world change begins.

HOW A LEADER RECEIVES A VISION

FIRST, LET'S DEFINE VISION. I've heard dozens of definitions and so have you. But my best shot at a crisp definition is this: *Vision is a picture of the future that produces passion.*

For Henry Ford it was the picture of a future where a Model T was parked in the driveway of every butcher, baker, and candlestick maker. For Dr. Martin Luther King Jr. it was the picture of a future where two children, one black and one white, would sit across from each other on a seesaw, oblivious of the color of each other's skin. Dr. Billy Graham pictured thousands of wayward people coming forward to trust Christ as the choir sang "Just As I Am."

For each of these people, their picture of the future made their hearts beat fast and their minds race. What picture does that to you?

Is it a picture of hungry children being fed and protected in a secure environment? Is it a picture of homeless people finding shelter or of abused women finding a safe place? Is it a picture of dying churches experiencing renewal? Confused people coming to faith? Lay people finding meaningful ministry opportunities? Does the thought of lonely people finding community in small groups or artists finally using their God-given gifts in church ministry bring a lump to your throat? I believe there are as many passion-producing pictures as there are leaders.

I WAS BORN FOR THIS!

WHEN GOD FINALLY BRINGS clarity of vision to a leader's life, everything changes. The dominoes start to fall. Here's the typical progression:

First, a leader *sees* the vision, sees that life-changing image of the future that makes his or her pulse quicken. Seeing the vision might be the result of reading Scripture or of hearing an exciting story of life-transformation. It might result from coming face-to-face with a need that grips one's heart. It might even come as a leading directly from God. More likely, though, one sees the vision through witnessing or experiencing a work of God that's already being done by someone else. Seeing this form of ministry or service ignites an internal response that simply can't be ignored.

Without hesitation the leader says, "I think I could give my life to this. I think maybe I was born for this!" Sometimes a vision comes like an epiphany, all at once—Bang!—it's there. Sometimes it comes into focus piece by piece over a long period of time, like a confusing puzzle that finally makes sense. But at some point a leader sees clearly the vision that God intends for him or her to see.

Then, almost immediately, comes the *feeling* of the vision. Remember our working definition: *Vision is a picture of the future that produces passion.* What makes a vision so powerful? It's not just the picture of the future. It's the energy and the passion it evokes deep in one's heart. This level of energy or passion must be experienced to be fully understood.

Almost thirty years ago, while Dr. B was casting his vision of life in a biblically functioning community, I experienced an intensity of emotion I'd never felt before in my life. Sometimes I felt like cheering wildly and at other times I felt like sobbing. Occasionally I wanted to stand up in front of my classmates and scream, "Hey, everybody, this is it! Don't you see it? Can't you feel it? The local church is the hope of the world. It's the God-ordained redemptive agency upon which the destiny of the entire world hangs. So cancel your career plans. Do something important with your one and only life. Lay it down for Christ and his church!" Decades have passed, but the feelings behind those words are as real to me today as they were in that college classroom.

And still today, if you strapped a heart monitor to my chest when someone is talking about the beauty, the power, or the potential of the church, it would beep and flash and smoke and signal:

Danger, Danger, Danger. After all these years, the passion isn't fading. On the contrary, it's growing in intensity. I've learned firsthand that God-given visions pack a powerful punch and make a lasting impact.

JUST GET ME GOING ON THE LOCAL CHURCH

RECENTLY, A WILLOW CREEK ASSOCIATION pastor in Canada invited me to speak at the tenth anniversary of his church. I felt honored and accepted his invitation. On the evening of the event, shortly before it was my turn to speak, a woman went to the platform to tell her story. She said that she had spent most of her years far from God. Her life journey had been marked by disillusionment, immorality, and brokenness. Then she said, "But someone invited me to this church, and I felt accepted here so I kept coming back. The services were so creative and the sermons were so relevant that I couldn't help but listen. Then I heard the gospel and learned that I was loved in spite of my waywardness and sin." Then she told us about her salvation experience, her spiritual growth, her involvement in a small group, and her discovery and development of her spiritual gift.

By the time she sat down, I was a basket case. Her experience of radical life-transformation was a perfect reflection of the pulse-quickening picture I had carried in my heart for so many years.

I tracked her down right after the service. I was more than a little misty-eyed while I thanked her for her words. My heart was crying out, *You personify what my whole life is about. I'd have given everything I am and have to hear one story like yours.*

Several weeks later I received a call from a congregation that was dreaming of buying land. They had the parcel picked out; all they needed was the money to pay for it. Inspired by their vision and their enthusiasm, I agreed to speak at their fund-raising dinner. During the first part of the program, members of the church took the microphone and talked about what their church meant to them. Later the congregation joined together in song and in prayer, praising God and asking for his blessing and guidance as they moved forward with their building project.

As I listened, I was reminded of Willow's early adventures when we were dreaming of purchasing land and building our first building. When it came time for me to speak I sensed the Holy Spirit telling me to "forget my script," so I scrapped my notes and spent the next twenty minutes just challenging people. "Give your life to this," I implored them. "Give all the money you can give. Give all the service you can give. Give all the prayers you can give. Give whatever you have to give, because for all eternity you'll look back over your shoulder and be glad you did."

When I finished my passionate plea and returned to my seat, the pastor's wife, who was sitting next to me at the table, patted me on the shoulder as if to say, "Are you okay? Do you need anything? Should we call 911?"

I don't know how to explain the depth of feeling stirred in me by the ongoing wonder of Acts 2 churches. I can't count how many times I've fallen on my knees after a ministry event at Willow or elsewhere and said to God, "Nothing else does this to me. Clearly I was born for this."

Can you see how vision and passion are inextricably bound together in the life of a leader? When God gives you a vision you'll know it. You'll see it clearly and feel it deeply.

A LEADER'S PASSION IS CONTAGIOUS

LEADERS ARE NOT THE only ones who are energized by the passion of their vision. Followers thrive on it. Whenever I hear a leader communicating a passionate, heartfelt, God-honoring vision I am energized whether I want to be or not. Recently at the end of a Willow Creek Arts Conference, Nancy Beach, our director of creative programming, presented her vision to the audience of artists who were gathered. Passionately she urged them to use their gifts and develop their skills to advance the cause of God's Kingdom. "Throw yourselves and your artistic talents into the local church," she said. "Don't hold anything back."

Having been unable to attend that session, I watched the video in my study a week later. The clarity of Nancy's vision and the depth of her passion made me want to sign up! I had to restrain myself from going home and running up to the attic to dig out my twelve-string guitar. Fortunately, better judgment prevailed (no church would benefit from my musical contribution). But such is the power of vision and passion.

Leaders should never apologize for the strength of feeling that accompanies their God-given visions. God designed leaders to experience their longing, their desire, and their drive deeply, and to express it fully. And when they do, they energize others.

TAKING RESPONSIBILITY

SO FIRST, LEADERS SEE the vision. Then they feel so deeply about it that they inspire others. The next step in the progression is for leaders to take responsibility for the vision. They have to own it.

In Acts 20:24, the apostle Paul says, "I consider my life worth nothing to me, if only I may finish the race and complete the task the Lord Jesus has given me." What is Paul saying? I think he's saying, "The moment I received my vision from God, fulfilling that vision became the pressing priority of my life. Whatever personal agenda I had has given way to the marching orders I received from God." Paul took that vision as far as any leader can—to his death. When God asks leaders to subordinate their own personal agendas to fulfill the visions he has given them, he knows that if they do that they will never be sorry. However, some of the most exciting visions that God ever offered to humans have languished, withered, and died. Why? Because some leader somewhere saw it and felt it but did not have the guts to own it or act on it. He or she failed to pursue it, so the vision never became reality.

I can only imagine what this does to the heart of God. Visions are priceless. They are holy entrustments from God that must be taken seriously. To squander a vision is an unthinkable sin.

Think of what our world would be like if Billy Graham had said, "No thanks, God. The vision sounds too costly. I'd like an easier assignment."

Imagine the life-change that never would have occurred if Chuck Colson, who started Prison Fellowship, had said, "Why should I waste my time on a bunch of social misfits and common criminals who have nothing to offer me? I prefer the perks of a private law practice."

Consider what would have been lost if Bob Pearce, the founder of World Vision, had said, "Let the hungry children starve to death. What can one man do, anyway?"

Closer to home, I shudder to think what my life would have been like if Dr. B had ignored his God-given vision of transforming the minds and hearts of college students by challenging them to build local churches.

Please don't miss this. If God has given you a kingdom vision, if you see it clearly and feel it deeply, you had better take responsibility for it. You had better give your life to it. That's why God made you a leader. That's your unique calling. That's what you and I will be held accountable for someday.

MAXIMIZING A LEADER'S RECEPTIVITY

I'VE OFTEN TALKED TO leaders who are frustrated by their inability to gain clarity about their vision from God. As I've compared their stories with the stories of leaders who have received clear visions from God, I've discovered a number of "conditions of heart" that seem to maximize our ability to hear and receive a vision from God. So now when I talk to a leader who is hesitant or unclear about his or her vision I ask the following questions:

- Have you yielded yourself fully enough to God?
- Have you asked God to unveil his vision for your life, or are you asking him to bless a plan that you've already come up with? We must come to God with empty hands and an open heart and ask, "What is your vision for my life?"
- Have you fasted?
- Have you prayed?
- Have you been quiet and waited on God in solitude?
- Have you cleaned up sinful patterns in your life?
- Have you weeded out the distractions and ambient noise that would keep you from hearing what God is trying to say to you?
- Have you read avidly? Have you traveled widely? Have you visited a variety of ministries around the world? Have you exposed yourself to the kaleidoscope of visions that God has given to others so that you can be inspired by the variety of options? If not, get out there! See what God is doing!

Receiving a vision from God is both a deeply spiritual thing and a deeply practical thing. It involves the quiet, internal work of making your heart ready, and also the energetic, external work of exploring and experimenting. Leaders must devote themselves to both efforts, trusting that their spiritual discipline and their hard work will be rewarded with a vision that will impassion them and inspire others.

COMMUNICATE VISION BY EMBODYING IT

AFTER A LEADER RECEIVES and owns a vision, the next challenge is to communicate it to others. What good is a vision unless a leader can help others to see it? But how? How does a leader best communicate a vision?

By embodying it. By personifying it. By living it out.

Former president Jimmy Carter did this as well as any leader I've ever seen. After his term as president of the United States, he desperately wanted Americans to catch the vision of providing quality housing for under-resourced people. Rather than immediately hitting the speaking circuit, he and his wife, Rosalyn, bought hammers and started hitting nails for Habitat for Humanity.

After months of embodying the vision, during which the entire nation had seen him swinging a hammer on the evening news— *then* he started giving talks about it. And people listened. How could they not listen to a man who had calluses on his hands from living out the picture God had painted in his mind?

By embodying his vision, Jimmy Carter was also making it clear that even if no one else joined him, he was going to bring his vision to life. We all communicate our vision most powerfully when we can look our friends and other potential followers in the eye and say, "I am giving my life to the fulfillment of this vision. I'd love to have you help me. But even if you don't, I am going to do what God has called me to do. One way or another, I am going to make this vision happen." That's probably why I love the song "I Have Decided to Follow Jesus." The second verse says, "Though none go with me, still I will follow." When I sing those words, I sing with enormous intensity. I mean them down to my toes.

In the twenty-seven years since the beginning of Willow, staff members have come and gone, board members have come and gone, elders have come and gone, key lay leaders and donors have come and gone. Most left because of the sad but unavoidable transitions dictated by a mobile society. Other departures were painful and cut me to the core. But either way, these exits have led to some of the loneliest moments of my life. Why? Because losing great people who shared my vision was always frustrating and disappointing—and sometimes downright scary. *How can I carry on the vision without this person?* I would wonder.

But I never ask myself that question anymore. After numerous late-night gut checks, I have come to complete clarity on this issue: By God's grace, I fully intend to pursue the vision God has entrusted to me, no matter what, no matter who comes or goes. I will not let the opinions of others affect my own commitment to God's call on my life. Whether Willow is setting records and I am enjoying enthusiastic support or if Willow is stumbling and bumbling and I end up alone, still I will pursue the vision. "Though none go with me, still I must follow." I am called to this vision. I must embody it. I *must*. It's a private thing between God and me.

Every church, every team, every organization demands and deserves a "vision embodier," someone whose life values and commitments personify the vision. Cut them and they bleed the vision. Mother Teresa did this for her order of nuns. She lived in the slums and cradled the dying in her arms until her own death. If people wanted to know what her vision was all about they had only to watch her for a day.

Your people need that kind of leadership from you. Willow people need it from me. They've got to see me embody the vision, they've got to see me live it out, every day.

COMMUNICATE VISION ONE-ON-ONE

THE SECOND WAY TO communicate a vision (in order of importance) is one-on-one vision casting. Jesus frequently used this approach. When he invited his disciples to join his kingdom vision, he talked to them individually, then looked them straight in the eye and asked, "Will you leave everything and join me?"

When one who has embodied a vision stands in a parking lot or looks across the table in a restaurant or sits on the tailgate of a pickup truck and casts a vision to someone else—one on one— look out. There is tremendous power in that. The most effective leaders I've ever known have a lock on this. Check their day-timers and you'll see scores of private interactions scheduled over breakfast, lunch, and dinner hours. During such meetings seasoned leaders carefully, passionately, and personally explain their vision, then they courageously ask individuals to join them.

And it does take courage. It isn't easy to make what I call the "big ask." Every leader knows the pain of having a respected friend or colleague dismiss their dream or question the validity of their vision. Occasionally that happens to even the best leaders, and every time it does it feels like rejection. But leaders need to ask anyway. "Fred, will you help us? Sally, we could use your expertise. Frank, we need a piece of equipment that you could provide. Dan, we'd love to have you join our board. Mary, I need a senior staff position filled and I think you could handle it."

Sometimes our "big ask" requires a person to trade a lucrative position in the marketplace for a lower-paying ministry role or move from a city they love or accept a challenge that stretches their gifts further than they think they can go. Leaders need to acknowledge the sacrifice involved. "I know this is no small thing I'm asking. Would you just pray about it? I'll pray too." From that point on, the decision is in God's hands and the leader must be willing to trust God for the outcome. But we must not let the fear of a person's refusal keep us from asking.

COMMUNICATING VISION BY GOING PUBLIC

THE LAST STEP IN communicating a vision is to cast the vision publicly, to speak to the whole church, the whole department, or the whole team. This is a daunting challenge because it forces leaders to put precise wording to their passions. It can also be nerve-wracking because every leader knows that the words he or she is bursting to say may well be received negatively. While opposition is hard enough to deal with in one-on-one situations, it is far more difficult when a group is involved and there is the very real possibility of causing division.

This is why some leaders choke and decide not to take that risk. They don't give the vision talk. They don't paint the passion-producing picture. They intentionally stay out of harm's way and acquiesce to the status quo—all to avoid possible pain. How tragic (and gutless, I might add). Everybody loses when a church's vision remains fuzzy. Everybody pays for the leader's lack of courage.

THE IMPORTANCE OF WHAT HAPPENS BEHIND THE SCENES

LET ME SUGGEST A way to bolster a leader's courage and also build consensus before taking a vision public. First, the leader brings together whoever makes up the senior leadership team of the church: key staff members, lay leaders, elders, deacons, and so on. Then he or she says to this group, "Our people deserve clarity on the vision God has given us. They need to know what we're about and where we're headed. So let's meet for the next eight Saturday mornings and figure out together, under the direction of the Holy Spirit, where God wants us to lead this church.

"We'll start by studying Acts 2 and asking God to give us the pictures, ideas, and words that capture his vision for this church. Then when we present it publicly we will be of one heart and one mind, and hopefully, the rest of the congregation will buy in. If some people don't resonate with the vision, we can talk to them one-on-one and give them time to process the potential changes. If after that they decide not to join us, we will trust that there are other churches where they will feel more at home. But let's come to leadership consensus so we can present the clearest, strongest vision possible."

I've seen hundreds of churches all over the world work through this process. Though it requires a major investment of time and energy, and things may get a bit bumpy along the way, the pay-off is huge. Inevitably there comes that day when the whole leadership core is united and clear about its vision. At that time, the point leader can communicate the vision to the entire congregation with passion and power. And if God has truly guided the process, the vision will ignite the church. People will say, "Finally we are not just doing laps. We have a course, we have a target, and we are free to move together into a God-honoring future."

REMEMBER THAT THE "WHO" AND THE "WHEN" MATTER

LET ME OFFER A few more tips about communicating the vision publicly. The "who" matters. By that I mean that choosing the appropriate person to give the talk is very important. Around Willow Creek we are totally committed both to team leadership and to team teaching. But when it comes to who will stand in front of the Willow Creek congregation on Vision Night and articulate what we're about and where we're headed, we don't draw straws. We believe that job is the responsibility of the recognized point leader, the person responsible for overseeing the team, congregation, or organization.

At Willow, that would be me. Many times I've suggested to the elders and management team that we let someone else handle that responsibility, but they don't even let me finish my spiel. "It's your job, Bill," they are quick to remind me. "You're the person who has embodied the vision from the beginning. You're the one whose passion we need to see and hear and experience again and again. The congregation needs to know that you are still committed to this dream and still willing to lay your time and energy on the line for it." The "who" matters. Churches must think this through and get it right.

The "when" also matters. In my experience, there are starting points, midway points, and ending points in a ministry season that almost demand a vision talk. In the United States, and particularly in the Midwest, our ministry season tends to run from September to Christmas. There's a brief Christmas break, when people are focused on family, travel, and holiday events, but then it typically fires up again from January to the end of June. The months of July and August, prime vacation months for Americans, force a natural lull in ministry momentum.

So, with these seasons in mind, I start the new ministry year with a vision talk in early September. Then in January, I do another vision talk. One January I did a vision talk called *The Soul of Willow Creek*. I delivered it at our weekend services because I wanted everyone, including seekers, to know who we are and where God is leading us. I wanted to give them a glimpse into the soul of Willow.

People loved it.

Two weeks later, at our midweek New Community services, we had our formal Vision Night where I recast the vision in greater detail. When I'm asked how often the vision should be publicly shared in an organization or in a church, I usually remind leaders that vision *leaks*. Most leaders think that if they fill people with vision once, they'll stay full forever. But that's just not true. Vision leaks, even out of our best people. The demands of everyday life gradually cause their minds to grow fuzzy, their commitment to wane, and their hearts to grow cold.

Effective leaders are always monitoring vision leakage. They stand ready to recast the vision whenever necessary. Most leaders, frankly, don't cast the vision enough. They blame followers for faltering commitment, not realizing that they have faltered in their role of vision caster.

PEOPLE NEED TO KNOW THE MAIN THING

ONE MORE PIECE OF counsel about going public with the vision: Keep it simple. What I'm saying here might be a tad controversial, but I've thought a lot about this. These days so much is being written about the technical distinctions between vision, mission, and purpose that some leaders feel compelled to have separate statements for each. For years, we too attempted to make these distinctions. But in the end, I think it produced more confusion than clarity in our congregation. People would say, "What's our vision? Oh, I thought that was our purpose. No that was our mission. I give up!"

To avoid this kind of mess, leaders should remember this simple rule. *When a leader is casting vision publicly the goal is to help people to know, understand, and remember the "main thing."*

Call it vision, purpose, mission, or whatever. But people better be able to walk away saying, "I know the main thing." At Willow Creek the main thing has always been "to turn irreligious people into fully devoted followers of Christ." And I don't ever want anybody at Willow to get fuzzy on this.

Peter Drucker says the main thing should be able to fit on the front of a T-shirt. That means it better be crisp. It better be repeatable. It better be the kind of statement the average layperson can recite back with minimal trouble. If it's a paragraph long, it's probably not repeatable. It has to be succinct and memorable. That's why we have stuck with the nine words we came up with twenty-seven years ago: *Turning irreligious people into fully devoted followers of Christ.*

VISION INCREASES ENERGY AND MOVES PEOPLE INTO ACTION

Sounds like a lot of work, doesn't it—crafting a rally cry? Maybe you're reading this and wondering if, after all the effort, anything would really be different? It's a fair question. "What will improve if I get clear on our vision and communicate it compellingly to my people?"

Let me frame it this way. Most churches are full of wonderful, good-hearted people (better than some of us leaders, for sure). But life has a way of sucking the zest out of them. Careers, kids, responsibilities, and financial pressures combine to overload them physically and emotionally. Eventually life begins to feel to them like a backbreaking grind. The last thing they want to do is add serving at church to their to-do list. But an energizing, God-honoring vision can change all that. I've seen it happen many times at Willow. I saw it happen again just recently.

I met a twenty-something guy who told me how dull his life had become. He had been hanging around at Willow, but he hadn't gotten plugged in anywhere. Then he heard Sue Miller, our director of children's ministry, cast her vision about ministering to kids. He heard her speak of how noble it is to serve and love kids, to lead them to Christ, and then to grow them up in faith. She challenged people to give their lives to nurturing and developing children. The vision she cast about the value of kids ignited this young man into action. Now he's a committed volunteer in *Promiseland,* our children's ministry.

I bumped into him a month after our first meeting and he was lit up like a Christmas tree. He described the eight kids in his *Promiseland* small group. He knew their names, their families, their stories. Now his life is far from dull.

The same thing happened recently when I ran into a couple in the hallway outside my office. They said, "We were around Willow for years, attending but not doing much else. Then we heard a leader in the small groups ministry cast a vision about the value of community and about what it would mean to invest our lives in shepherding a small group of people."

They were so energized by that vision that they went through the training to become small group leaders. With great animation they said, "Our lives now revolve around leading our small group. It's the most important and exciting thing we do."

That's the power of vision. It creates energy that moves people into action. It puts the match to the fuel that most people carry around in their hearts and yearn to have ignited. But we leaders must keep striking that match by painting compelling kingdom pictures. Again, the leadership gift is the only gift that provides this energizing spark for the church. So we need to get this right.

VISION INCREASES OWNERSHIP

THE SECOND PAYOFF OF casting vision effectively is increased ownership. One of my fears related to vision is that someday our key leaders—board members, elders, management team, and lay leaders—will hear of an upcoming Vision Night and they'll yawn and say, "Been there, heard that."

But the truth is, whenever I recast the vision to Willow, not only will new folks resonate, respond, and make our vision theirs, but inevitably, the faithful core upon whose shoulders Willow has been carried for so long will enthusiastically recommit. Veterans often make their way down to the bullpen where I stand after services and say, "Sign me up for another year. You can count on me. I'm more motivated by what we're doing together as a church than I ever have been before. I can't bear the thought of missing any part of the action." Seeing the clear picture again deepens their sense of ownership.

After a recent vision talk one of the founders of Willow, a man who's seen and heard it all, approached me and, with his finger to my chest, announced, "Bill, they're gonna have to take me out of here in a box." Translated: "I'm going to give the rest of my life to the vision of this church. I'm not going anywhere. I'm not going to lose heart. If the battle gets hard, I'm not going to quit. I'm here 'til the end. You can count on me." A commitment like that is one of the results of effective vision casting.

VISION PROVIDES FOCUS

A THIRD BENEFIT OF vision casting is that it provides focus. A clear articulation of what a particular church is about also offers, by implication, a clear statement about what it *isn't* about. In other words, every vision that is cast embraces certain essential activities, but it also excludes scores of other energy-diverting activities. These excluded activities may be good in and of themselves, but if they are unrelated to the specific vision of a particular church, pursuing them will do more harm than good. Nothing neutralizes the redemptive potential of a church faster than trying to be all things to all people. It is impossible for any one church to do it all.

Leaders at Willow have been asked hundreds of times why we have never started a Christian day school. Our answer has remained the same from the beginning: we have never sensed God's prompting to head down that road. That being the case, we have been able to focus with greater intensity on evangelism and discipleship, both of which we have clearly sensed to be closer to the bull's-eye of God's vision for us.

A clear vision provides a compelling picture of the future that enables us to say, "We know our destination. Nothing will lure us off the path from here to there. We will not be distracted."

Leaders who realize the importance of actualizing their church's collective vision will unapologetically say "no" to all sorts of competing endeavors. Why? So that someday they can hear these words: "You stayed true to the vision I gave you. You didn't get sidetracked. You reached the unique destination I had in mind for your church. Well done! Well done!"

VISION SMOOTHS LEADERSHIP SUCCESSION

So THE PAYOFFS OF a clearly defined vision are increased energy, increased ownership, and increased focus. Without being morbid, allow me to mention just one final payoff of painting a clear vision for the church: it reduces the trauma of leadership succession.

I won't be the senior pastor of Willow Creek forever. The human death rate still hovers around a hundred percent, and I doubt that I will be an exception to that statistic. Neither will you. So, we both need to understand that one of the greatest gifts we leaders can give our churches is a clear, God-honoring vision that will outlast us. Someday the elders of Willow Creek will begin the search for the next senior pastor. I fully expect that they will approach the candidates and say, "Here's what Willow is about. Here's the picture that produces passion at Willow. Here's the main thing that God has assigned us to do.

"We are a church with a white-hot commitment to turning irreligious people into fully devoted followers of Christ. We're united around that vision. We're energized by it. We own it. And we have laser-like focus. So if our vision and your vision are in sync and God leads you to become our next senior pastor, all you'll have to do is step into place, keep the rockets lit, and have a ball flying with us into the future."

Wouldn't that be a wonderful way to pass a leadership baton? Wouldn't the bride of Christ be well served if we could sustain vision even during leadership transitions?

But what happens in most churches? Every four or five years, there's a ninety-degree vision change when a new pastor comes. Long-time church members know deep down that "this too shall pass." No wonder they eventually cross their arms and say, "We're not going to get on board with this vision. Before we even figure out what it means there will probably be a new one in place. Why should we bother to get serious about it?" I've seen entire congregations commit themselves to noninvolvement because of their frustration with revolving-door pastors and shifting visions. And I can't say I blame them.

But it doesn't have to be this way. Just as clear vision creates energy, increases ownership, and provides focus, it can also help churches maintain momentum and effectiveness during the critical process of passing the baton from one leadership team to the next.

A PAYOFF WRITTEN ON FACES

A FEW YEARS AGO I asked our video team to tape the part of our baptism service where new adult believers are immersed in the lake on our church property. With a song written by one of our vocalists used as background music, the video team created a three-minute video clip that is the most moving celebration of life transformation I have ever seen.

I decided to show the video at the annual Christmas party we have for our elders and board of directors. After enjoying a beautiful dinner I stood up and said, "Friends, I want to say thank you for serving for another year here. I want you to understand how very much I appreciate and love you. I thought the greatest gift I could give you tonight would be a visual image of the main thing that we're about. So just sit back and enjoy what you're going to see during the next few minutes."

Since I had already seen the video several times during the editing process, I was free to look into the faces of our senior leaders, those men and women who for so many years have carried heavy ministry loads with uncommon faithfulness. I wish you could have seen the energy, the joy, the determination, and the sense of fulfillment evident on their faces. I think their hearts were forming a silent choir singing, "Yes! This is our main thing. This is what God has called us to do. This is what we want to be about for the rest of our lives."

When the video clip ended, we looked into each other's tear-filled eyes and just sat there for several minutes in blissful silence, bathed afresh in God's vision for our church. It was the kind of moment leadership teams live for, the kind of moment only a crystal-clear vision can produce.

Vision. It's the most potent weapon in a leader's arsenal. It's the weapon that unleashes the power of the church.

CHAPTER THREE

Getting-It-Done Leadership

Turning Vision into Action

As we just learned, vision is a white-hot commodity. For a mature, effective leader, however, there is one thing even more exciting than clarifying and casting a God-honoring vision: achieving the vision. Forgive me if that seems elementary, but I run across an alarming number of leaders who would rather *cast* vision than roll up their sleeves and attempt, with the Spirit's power, to *achieve* it!

Such leaders eventually lose credibility. I've never known a leader who could keep the vision hot and the team motivated indefinitely without eventually being able to say to the troops, "We're making progress. That dream we've been dreaming, that prayer we've been praying, that picture of the future that's fired us up—well, it's happening. We're not just blowing smoke."

A leader who can't point to actual progress will eventually have to answer an awkward question from someone on the team: "Oh great Visionary One, when might we get some indication that we're getting closer to the destination?" A question like that should tip off a leader that teammates will not endure mere vision casting indefinitely. They need to see results.

IT TAKES MORE THAN ANOTHER PEP TALK

SOME LEADERS BELIEVE THAT the key to getting results is simply to cast the vision again ... and again ... and again. They are convinced that if they just keep talking about the dream and keep focused on the dream and keep people thinking and praying and pumped up about the dream, it will automatically happen. One bright morning everybody will wake up and find the entire vision actualized before their very eyes. Voila! Mission accomplished.

But accomplishing a vision requires a lot more than pep talks, slogans, emotional stories, and heart-tugging video clips. It's taken me the better part of twenty-seven years to figure this out, but I'm clear about it now. There's a huge difference between visionary leadership and getting-it-done leadership. Did I say huge?

To explain this, let me illustrate with a sailing story, actually with the first of what may seem like many sailing stories. While I've learned leadership lessons primarily in the church, I have also been challenged as a leader in my favorite recreational activity, sailboat racing.

A few summers ago I had the sailing opportunity of a lifetime. A businessman friend of mine allowed me to enter his half-million dollar sailboat in a regatta against seven other identical yachts. Not only were these race boats considerably larger—and way more expensive—than the boat I owned at the time, but they were crewed by some of the best professional sailors in the world. I knew that my regular crew and their leader (me!) were outclassed by miles, but after adding a few more experienced sailors to our crew we were convinced we were ready to take on the big boys.

The day before the regatta we went out to practice. I gave a little pep talk that went something like this, "Most of us will probably never, ever get another opportunity like we have this weekend. Several of our competitors are America's Cup sailors. Every boat out there has highly paid helmsmen and tacticians. We have the opportunity to prove that we can compete with the best of the best!"

On and on I went with a vision talk so inspiring I started to feel sorry for the competition.

So with high anticipation, we headed out into Lake Michigan to practice and get acclimated to the boat. None of us had ever sailed such a technically sophisticated boat, but we managed to master our upwind work quite quickly. With our adrenaline surging, we turned downwind and hoisted the huge, colorful spinnaker. It was a blustery day on Lake Michigan, and before long we were surfing down the backsides of the waves, spewing white sheets of spray on either side of the hull.

Fueled by the power and excitement of it all, the crew went nuts. We were all high-fiving each other and talking about how we were going to kick the posteriors off the America's Cup guys. At that point, we were not having a confidence problem.

Then, in winds of nearly thirty knots, we attempted to jibe the huge spinnaker from one side of the boat to the other. This required teamwork like we had never experienced on our much smaller boat. It required complex timing sequences and perfect in-sync coordination by all thirteen members. Good thing we were pumped up and ready.

But our first jibe did not go well. The scene of an airplane crash comes to mind. Halfway through it, we fouled up everything. The second jibe did not go well either. Nor did the third, the fourth, the tenth, or the twentieth. When we ended practice that day, we had not completed one single race-worthy jibe. And the race was the next day.

In the morning, before heading out to the race course for a little more practice, I had a very important leadership decision to make. I had the option of giving another vision talk, a pep-'em-up, psych-'em-up, let's-go-out-and-beat-those-America's-Cup-guys speech. I could pour more emotional fuel on their fires and hope it would work. Or . . . I could take an entirely different approach.

I chose to do the latter. I gathered the crew together and said, "No pep talk this morning. I think we all know that this is the opportunity of a lifetime. I don't think any of us lack commitment or enthusiasm for this regatta. What we have to do in this brief practice is learn how to execute a few basic maneuvers. So let's sit down and talk it through. Before we even leave the dock, let's talk through who is doing what on the jibes. How can we work together better? How can we get on the same page? If we don't do that, we can kiss this regatta good-bye, and I, for one, am not prepared to do that."

Then I asked the best sailor on our team, someone who's much more skilled than I am, to do something with the crew that most of those guys had not been subjected to since they were beginning sailors. I asked him to walk us through the spinnaker jibing sequence before we even put up the sail.

So, here we are, in a half-million dollar racing boat, still at the dock next to the America's Cup professionals, going through elementary lessons in sailing. Slowly and deliberately, as if we were the dullest crayons in the box, our crew chief explained, "This-is-a-spinnaker-pole. This-is-the-foreguy. This-is-the-guy. This-is-the-topping-lift."

He continued his lesson, "Now, when we jibe from port to starboard, here's the sequence." He talked everybody through the entire sequence step-by-step. Then he made us practice each step. He did it repeatedly until we had the maneuver down cold.

Nearing race time, we threw off the dock lines and motored out of the harbor. When we were clear of the breakwater we hoisted the spinnaker and called for a real jibe. To our great relief, we executed it perfectly. Morale shot through the roof. Then we did another and another. Long story short, throughout the entire regatta, we never missed a spinnaker jibe.

That's not to say we did that great against the competition. How else can I say it? Those America's Cup guys are really good.

We lost the regatta, but I gained a valuable lesson in leadership that has served me well ever since. Namely, that at a certain point *people need more than vision. They need a plan, a step-by-step explanation of how to move from vision to reality.*

REFINING VISION WITH A STRATEGIC PLAN

AT WILLOW, WE HAVE invested lots of energy in trying to discover how to do this in an Acts 2 church. In fact, in the mid-nineties we decided to formally draft and implement a strategic plan.

But this presented a problem. I had never gone through a strategic planning process, not in my business days before entering the ministry, not in youth ministry days, not in all the years of Willow. I sensed it had to be done, but I didn't know how to do it. Fortunately, I was able to lean heavily on our executive pastor, Greg Hawkins, who had considerable expertise in that area. Over a six-months period, he and his team led us through a process that involved, among other things, refining our vision.

We started by re-examining "the main thing." After many months of meetings with staff, boards, elders, and key lay leaders, we concluded that God was still calling us to do the main thing he had called us to do from the beginning of Willow: turn irreligious people into fully devoted followers of Christ.

But we also felt that we needed to refine our vision, particularly for internal leadership purposes. After extensive discussion, we decided to highlight three areas of emphasis within our broader vision.

The first emphasis was evangelism. We decided that for the next five years we would actively focus on reaching a higher percentage of people in the Chicago area with the gospel.

Our second emphasis was the spiritual maturity of our believers. We would encourage full devotion to Christ by lifting up the values of community, spiritual growth, and full participation in the life of the church.

For the third emphasis we determined to invest more of ourselves, our knowledge, and our resources outside the walls of Willow Creek Community Church. We looked to both our Extension Ministries, which serve those living in conditions of poverty, and the Willow Creek Association, which serves local churches throughout the world, to spearhead this thrust.

As a younger church we had done fine with a broad mission statement. But to challenge a maturing church, we had to add greater definition and more strategic focus to that broad statement.

After months of meeting and discussing and drafting potential statements, each of our leadership bodies signed off on our five-year strategic plan. At that point we thought we were ready to present the plan to the entire staff and congregation.

But something told us we weren't done yet. We had not completed our job. We felt the Spirit of God prompting us to set specific goals in conjunction with our refined vision.

SETTING GOALS WITH BALANCE IN MIND

CONFESSION: FOR THE FIRST twenty years of Willow we never formalized any specific goals. We had stayed focused on our vision and had seen thousands of lives transformed. So why mess with goals? But as we prayed about it, we sensed new direction from the Holy Spirit. We concluded that we would never become the kind of church we hoped to be at the end of five years without specific goals to help us get there.

Yes, we were going to focus on evangelism. And help our believers mature. And invest more of our resources outside the church. But what were the specifics? How much energy should we put into each of those objectives? What percentage of our resources should go outside the walls of Willow? What would help us stay balanced, whole, and healthy in the years ahead?

As I've traveled around the world I've seen a lot of unbalanced churches. Some do evangelism very effectively, but they don't disciple new believers. Other churches are great when it comes to teaching and preaching but ignore the value of community and do nothing with small groups. Some churches focus on both evangelism and discipleship, but they don't address the needs of an aching world; they don't care for the poor. We wanted to be sure that as we grew we would come ever closer to the perfect balance of the Acts 2 church.

SIX "BIG, HAIRY, AUDACIOUS GOALS" – WILLOW STYLE

BUT HOW WOULD WE know if we were moving toward that vision if we didn't set mile markers along the way? How could we chart our progress? For the first time in twenty years our leadership circles thought, prayed, and wrestled through the process of setting specific goals. We decided on six goals that corresponded to our three strategic emphases.

The goals were big—scary big!

In his book *Built to Last*, Jim Collins talks about BHAGs: Big, Hairy, Audacious Goals. We decided we wanted our goals to be big enough to require the supernatural activity of God. We wanted to set goals that would keep us on our knees.

After more meetings and late-night prayer sessions, we informed our congregation of our five-year goals.

To reach our *first emphasis* of extending the gospel to more people in the Chicago area we established this goal:

1. To increase attendance at our four weekend seeker services from 15,000 people to 20,000 people. We knew that figure would optimize our seating capacity.

To accomplish the *second emphasis* of maturing our believers we focused on these goals:

2. To have one hundred percent participation in small groups. At that time, approximately half of our weekend attendees were in small groups, and we were not satisfied with that. We hoped that if we were eventually blessed with a congregation of 20,000, all 20,000 people would be enjoying small group community.

3. To increase attendance at our midweek New Community services from 4,000 to 8,000. These services, which meet on Wednesday and Thursday evenings, offer deeper teaching and corporate worship, both necessary components in spiritual growth.

4. To encourage each of our 8,000 potential midweek attendees to become fully participating members of the church. This would mean that each individual would be engaged in a disciplined growth process, volunteering in some area of service, and giving financially to God's work.

For our *third emphasis* of investing ourselves, our knowledge, and our resources outside the walls of Willow we set the following goals:

5. To have 4,000 of our people serving those who live in conditions of poverty at least once a year. This might mean building houses with Habitat for Humanity or working with one of our ministry partners in downtown Chicago or doing a short-term assignment in Mexico or the Dominican Republic. Because we really didn't know what to expect in this regard, we almost randomly set this number.

6. To increase from 1,400 to 6,000 the number of domestic and international churches ministered to by the Willow Creek Association.

FINDING CHAMPIONS

ANNOUNCING OUR GOALS PUBLICLY drove us to our knees with renewed fervor. We felt challenged, nervous, and excited about them all at the same time. We were more aware than ever that they were, indeed, BHAGs—big, hairy, audacious goals. That's when we realized we needed to take one more major step if we wanted to reach these goals.

Looking around our leadership circle, I asked, "Who among you would like to become a goal champion? Who is willing to commit the next five years of your life to providing leadership for the achievement of one of these goals?"

One by one, senior leaders stepped up.

"I have a heart that beats for evangelism," said one leader. "I would be willing to provide leadership in that area. I'll commit myself to raising the evangelistic temperature around here until someday we have 20,000 people at our weekend seeker services."

Another took on the challenge of the small groups goals. Someone else took responsibility for the midweek New Community goals. Pretty soon we had a champion for each of the six goals we had set.

Excitement began to build. I remember saying to our senior leaders one night, "Can you imagine what Willow will be like five years from now if, by God's power and our focused efforts, we actually reach these goals? We will be a thriving, growing, deepening, balanced, biblically functioning community of faith, the likes of which none of us have ever seen. Who wouldn't want to be a part of an adventure like this?"

NEW ENERGY, NEW EXCITEMENT: WILLOW RELAUNCHED

WE LAUNCHED THE STRATEGIC plan in January of 1996. I spelled it out to the congregation and could feel the temperature rising. Like the senior leaders, the congregation said, "Let the adventure begin. Let's go. Count us in. We'll do our part." In a way it felt like the relaunching of Willow. There was the same kind of excitement we had experienced during the early theater days.

As the months unfolded, I was delighted with the effect that our refined vision statement seemed to be having. I quickly became a major proponent of goals and measurable progress. We broke our five-year goals into twelve-month goals and started keeping track of our progress. A year into it we were able to say about some goal areas, "Yes! We're right on track with the plan. We are meeting our goals. Yea, God!"

But we could also see that we were falling behind in some other areas. That led to stimulating conversations at our leadership meetings. Our goal champions would say, "Hey, let's talk about this. What's the problem? Have we established unrealistic goals? Or are we just not praying earnestly enough or not thinking clearly enough? We are talking about the redemptive potential of the church. We've got to put our heads together and figure out what needs to be done."

It had been years since that kind of energy had been released in the leadership circles at Willow. I loved it. I fanned it. The management team kicked into a whole new level of leadership. We quickly covenanted to do everything in our power to make sure that all six goals were being achieved simultaneously. We made sure all six champions had access to the top leaders and resources of the church. The elders started giving their input and tracking our progress. The board of directors started discussing how they could provide dollars, facilities, and equipment to help us achieve the six goals.

I could sense us pulling together like I had rarely experienced in church leadership before. You could feel the synergistic energy. I thought, *This is fun. We have a refined vision. We have clear goals and goal champions. We have rising levels of energy, determination, and faith. What more could we as leaders do?*

ONE THING MISSING

As IT TURNED OUT, a lot more.

About sixteen months into this five-year plan, I started feeling an uneasiness that was hard to put into words. When I tried to explain it to the management team and elders, the best I could offer was a vague assessment: "Somehow it seems that we're still not hitting on all eight cylinders. We're hitting on four or five, but not on all eight. We're not all on the same page."

And they would say, "Bill, who isn't? What isn't firing right?" And I'd say, "I'm not sure. But I want to figure this thing out, and I need your help. Let's do it together."

I have to be honest; this was a stressful period for all of us in senior leadership at Willow. I was a gadfly, poking around and asking questions while everyone else was rolling their eyes and groaning, "There he goes again."

Then one night in my kitchen at home, I had an awakening. My then college-aged daughter, Shauna, was home from school on a break, and she had invited five or six friends over for dinner. I was standing in the kitchen talking to them when one of the girls began telling me how she had come to Christ through our high school ministry called Student Impact.

I have enormous respect for Student Impact—it helped my own kids immeasurably—so I was not surprised to hear about its impact on this young woman.

She continued to tell me that she was attending a college out east. When I asked her where she went to church out there, I expected her to say she was involved in a local church, maybe even in a Willow Creek Association Member Church. But she didn't say that. She said, "Well, I don't go to church out there."

I thought maybe she was having trouble relating to a more traditional church after coming to Christ at Willow. So I suggested that perhaps she was just in a period of transition and that it might take her a while to find another church. "But there are a lot of great churches out there," I added. "I'm sure you'll find something."

And she said, "Oh, I don't think that's it. I never was a part of Willow Creek Church, anyway. I just went to Student Impact."

"Really?" I said. "Then what church did you attend while you were in high school?"

"I never went to church," she admitted.

"Time out," I said, thinking that I had become completely lost somewhere in this conversation. "I thought you said you attended Student Impact for four years."

"That's right, I did," she smiled. "I found Christ there. I was discipled there. I learned to serve there. I just never heard much about Willow Creek Community Church."

My pulse quickened as I remembered conversations with a similar tone that I'd had recently with staff members in the hallways at Willow. "How is Willow doing with its strategic plan?" they'd ask. I remember thinking, *Why are you asking me how Willow is doing? Aren't you a part of Willow? Why aren't you asking me how we are doing with our goals? Aren't Willow's goals your goals?*

The more I thought about this "disconnect," the clearer it became to me. Over the years some things had changed at the church. Without my being consciously aware of it, Willow had evolved from a close-knit, single-identity, biblically functioning community into a decentralized, multi-identitied, loosely connected federation of sub-ministries. For many people, all they really knew of Willow was the sub-ministry to which they related. Even on staff, many people identified more strongly with the department they were working in than they did with the church as a whole.

That's why we don't all seem to be on the same page. We're not!

The problem with this was that not every sub-ministry was as committed as it needed to be to the goals of spiritual growth that we had agreed upon as a church.

I told the executive leadership team, "We need more than a refined vision statement, clear goals, and goal champions to achieve the full redemptive potential of this church. We need to connect every full- and part-time staff member directly to our strategic plan, and we need to retrain everyone to feel responsible for the future of the church as a whole, not just for their particular departments. Then maybe we'll start firing on all eight cylinders."

The executive leadership team agreed, but that didn't mean the problem had an easy fix. I realized we were going to have to do a variation of what my sailing buddy did with our racing team when we couldn't jibe the spinnaker. We had to go back to the basics.

CHURCH BASICS: ALIGNMENT

WE HAD TO SAY to the staff, "This-is-a-church. We-are-a-single-entity. We-are-a-biblically-functioning-community. We're-not-a-constellation-of-planets-revolving-around-a-central-mother-planet."

In other words, "Here is what Acts 2 says. Here is what it means to be a church. Here is what we have to do to develop a radiant, flourishing bride of Christ. We all have to participate in this alignment challenge. How can we claim to be members of one body unless we are going in the same direction, pursuing the same goals?

"If we don't pull together, the health of Willow will slowly deteriorate. In time it will wither and die. We cannot let that happen."

I wish I could say that this staff alignment came off as smoothly as the jibes after our crew practice, but it just didn't happen like that. Some staff who had operated with enormous independence for a decade or more weren't too excited about having to modify their sub-ministry plans in order to put more energy into the wider church challenge. Some felt we were changing the rules in the middle of the game, and, in a way, we were.

For many years we had hired staff, given them budgets, and said, "Go build a single-adult ministry, build a youth ministry, build a music ministry. Have fun." And they were having a ball. But some of them were headed in dramatically different directions from the church at large. While they were all engaged in worthwhile endeavors, they were not all consistently moving the people in their ministries toward the goals we had agreed upon as a church. Some sub-ministries had no specific plans for helping people engage more consistently in spiritual disciplines or get involved in small groups or serve as ministry volunteers or reach out to the poor. How could we expect the congregation as a whole to move in those directions if the leaders of sub-ministries were not holding up those values? But when we said, "Now it's time for all of us to share a piece of what it means to build the whole church," some cried foul, and it got a little ugly.

Most of the staff were receptive and jumped on board as soon as they saw the issue. But for others, it was a long bumpy road, longer and bumpier than I ever anticipated. It took many months filled with meetings and discussions to help everybody see that a federation of sub-ministries was neither biblical nor sustainable.

DRAWING A LINE IN THE SAND

WHEN I SAY THE road was long and bumpy, I mean it. And it took a heavy emotional toll on me. In one staff meeting I had to resort to using a quote from Jack Welch, the crusty, hard-nosed former CEO of General Electric. He said that there are times when a leader "cannot be this thoughtful, in-the-corner-guru. You cannot be a moderate, balanced, thoughtful, careful articulator of policy. You've got to be on the lunatic fringe."[1]

That about captured my emotional state at this juncture. I was totally out of patience with trying to be calm and rational. At a critical point, after several months of talking through the staff alignment process, I finally said to the staff, "I'm done being cool, calm, and collected about this alignment process. The whole future of Willow is hanging in the balance. I am resolved that we are going to align ourselves with the God-anointed strategic plan of this church. Do you understand?

"If any of you feel disinclined to get on board with this plan, feel free to find another church ministry that you can fully support. No hard feelings, but it's a new day here."

I have never enjoyed resorting to the use of power in my position as a church leader. I know Jesus' warnings about wielding power. I recognize the danger. But I believe that there are times when a leader has to draw a line in the sand. There comes a time when an issue has been processed into oblivion, and a leader must take action.

[1]Robert Slater, *Jack Welch and the GE Way* (New York: McGraw-Hill, 1999), 42.

So I said to the staff, "I'm not asking for your begrudging participation in this alignment. I'm asking for your one hundred percent commitment to pray and work and serve toward the realization of this plan. It's one-hundred-percent time. If you can't give it, or won't give it, it's time for you to go. We need everybody's participation to reach our full potential as a church."

That day a number of staff members stopped carrying pictures of me in their wallets. But great credit goes to my senior colleagues for pulling together and redirecting every person, every position, every department in the church to reflect a total commitment to achieving our vision.

SHARING RESPONSIBILITY FOR THE WHOLE

THIS WAS ONE OF the most taxing leadership challenges we have ever experienced at Willow. But we stuck to it with relentless resolve, and I have no regrets. These days, every staff person holds a stake in the overall goals of the church. Each staff member carries responsibility for helping the church reach its strategic plan. Every department in the church is fueling the evangelistic flame so that we can fill our weekend services with seekers who are coming to Christ. Every department in the church is raising the value of community and drawing people into small groups. Every department of the church is challenging people to attend the New Community midweek services, to become participating members of the church, and to serve the poor and to serve churches around the world.

We now bring leaders from every department before the entire management team and elders twice a year to make formal presentations highlighting both their departmental progress and their efforts in helping the church attain its overall goals. Those three days of meetings are very intense, but also very exhilarating. I always go home from those sessions on an adrenaline high.

First Corinthians 14:40 says that in the church "everything should be done in a fitting and orderly way." I can finally read that verse without feeling guilty. I remember sitting in my car after the first round of department presentations, thinking, *We're finally providing decent leadership around here. And it's not just vision casting, pep talks, slogans, and power-point leadership. It's get-the-job-done leadership.*

A MODERN DAY TRAGEDY

I HAVE THE PRIVILEGE of visiting many churches, and I have noticed that many leaders have caught the excitement of vision casting. They stand before their congregations and say, "We're gonna take the world!" Then I visit the church three years later and they haven't taken a block. They haven't taken a sidewalk. If anything, they've lost ground. This is a kingdom tragedy.

I recently attended a funeral in a church I had visited nearly thirty years ago. As I sat in a pew toward the back I couldn't help but ponder the history of that church. From what I could see, little had changed in thirty years. According to the bulletin wedged in a wooden pocket on the back of the pew in front of me, there was still one Sunday morning service, where 175 people filled about two thirds of the available seating in that sanctuary.

I can't tell you how it grieved me to realize that there are approximately 10,000 more people in the community immediately surrounding that church than there were thirty years ago, but weekend attendance appears to be the same. *O God,* I thought, *where are the people whose lives could have been radically altered had someone brought them to church? What's happened to them during these years? Who is offering the message of hope to this community? Who is reaching out to neighbors, coworkers, and friends who are far from God?*

Why, I wondered, did the good people in this church settle for having such low impact in their community? Why did they let their church fall so short of its potential?

I think I would feel better about situations like this if I knew that church leaders had drafted bold plans, had done their best to implement them, and had prayed fervently for God's blessing, but then for some reason had failed miserably to reach their goals. At least there would have been honest effort. But rarely is that the case. Most often there is a faithful core of sincere believers who would love to help their church have greater impact, if they just knew what to do. But they don't. So they sit in their comfortable pews, frustrated as they watch a long line of pastors pass through the revolving doors, each devoted to God and willing to study and preach, but none, apparently, challenged or trained (or perhaps gifted) to exercise leadership.

These good people, and hundreds of thousands of others like them in churches all over the world, have never been led. They've been preached to and taught. They've been fellowshipped and Bible-studied. They've taken courses on prayer and evangelism. But with no one to inspire them, to mobilize them, and to coordinate their efforts, their desire to make a difference for Christ has been completely frustrated.

I believe that the great tragedy of the church in our time has been its failure to recognize the importance of the spiritual gift of leadership. It appears to me that only a fraction of pastors worldwide are exercising the spiritual gift of leadership, organizing the church around it, and deploying church members through it. The results, in terms of church growth and worldwide spiritual impact, are staggering.

We must understand what it means to the kingdom when leadership gifts are not exercised. Hebrews 13:17 reminds church leaders that we "must give an account" for what we do with our leadership gifts. Obviously there are negative consequences when any spiritual gift is neglected. Why, then, were those with the leadership gift singled out in this passage? I believe it's because the consequences of neglecting the leadership gift are so far-reaching. When those of us with leadership gifts fail to lead effectively, the entire local church is affected, not to mention the unchurched people in our communities.

The church must come to grips with the fact that the gift of leadership is the catalytic gift that energizes, directs, and empowers all the other gifts. People with the spiritual gift of leadership are called to nurture an environment where teachers can teach and shepherds can shepherd and administrators can administer. Without it, the other gifts languish, the church becomes inwardly focused and impotent, and unbelievers end up with a one-way, nonstop ticket to the abyss. That's why I underscore again what Paul so passionately said to leaders, "If you have the leadership gift ... LEAD!"

WHAT IT MEANS TO BE A DILIGENT LEADER

FOR YEARS I'VE BEEN trying to help people understand the importance of the spiritual gift of leadership.

My hope is that all leaders in the kingdom will commit themselves to fully developing their leadership potential. All leaders need to strive continually to lift their leadership capacity to the next level, no matter how difficult that is. We need to be willing to move out of our comfort zones, to learn new skills and disciplines, and even to submit to a process of retraining. I want to challenge all of us leaders to put ourselves on intense growth tracks, to read and reflect, to travel and seek training, to look for mentors, and to begin a nonstop search for the best leadership models we can find. I am asking leaders to be humble enough to learn. I am asking all of us leaders to be courageous enough to apply best practice in appropriate, Spirit-anointed ways in whatever leadership arena God assigns us.

I know that some people feel hesitant at this point. And I think it's a "fair ask" to wonder if this is what the Holy Spirit had in mind on Pentecost day when he blew life and power into the church and commissioned it to change the world. Did God have goals and strategic planning in mind as useful tools to serve the church's mission? Or are we just superimposing worldly business practices into the spiritual world where they don't belong? With our emphasis on leadership are we at risk of strategically planning the supernatural power of the Holy Spirit right out of the church?

These are critical questions. Leaders must decide where to settle on these issues. How seriously should we take leadership and management? How diligently should we try to convert vision into reality in the church? Should we just dream and give pep talks and leave the rest to God? Or should we manage for results?

HARD QUESTIONS AT HARVARD BUSINESS SCHOOL

I HAD TO ADDRESS these questions some years ago in a unique setting. I was at the Harvard Business School to defend the Willow Creek case study written by Jim Mellado, now the president of the Willow Creek Association but then a Harvard business student. After seeing how much attention we paid to leadership and management functions at Willow, one of the students raised his hand and challenged me.

"Bill, I just don't think you should mix best management practices with spiritual stuff." He continued, "I'm really uneasy with all this leadership training, leadership development, and managing for results that I see at Willow. I think that when it comes to God, the spiritual realm, and the church, it ought to be laissez-faire. Hands off. Let go and let God. That's what I think."

I scanned the expectant faces in that multi-tiered classroom and quickly prayed, "God, please help me to explain this well." Then I directed my attention back to my challenger. "You know, I find it very interesting that you're here in one of the best schools in the history of education, learning the very latest and greatest leadership and management disciplines so that you can graduate from here and join a secular company to help them set records manufacturing and selling widgets, soap, or software. There's nothing wrong with that. People can benefit from using all that stuff so you might as well do your best to get it into their hands. But still, it's only stuff. It isn't going to transform anybody's life in a deeply significant way. It isn't going to change the world or determine anybody's eternal destiny.

"What you have to understand is that some of us church leaders believe to the core of our beings that the local church is the hope of the world. We really believe that. We believe that the church is the only God-anointed agency in society that stewards the transforming message of the love of Christ. We believe that the church addresses every human being's deepest need. We believe that the church can lead people into a whole new way of living and loving and serving, and can thereby transform society.

"You also need to realize that some of us church leaders live daily with the realization that the eternal destinies of people in our communities hang in the balance. That's why we are so determined to get our visions right and live out our values and come up with effective strategies. We truly believe that it matters that we attain our goals. It matters that we align our staffs and leverage our resources. We believe that the success or failure of our churches directly affects people's lives here today and for eternity. We believe this to our depths. We'd take bullets for it."

I continued, "That's why we make no apology for learning and applying best practice principles as God leads us in our churches. How could we do otherwise? The church is the hope of the world."

It got very quiet in that room.

Later I thought about that moment. If I really believe that the church is the hope of the world then that has huge implications for my own spiritual gift of leadership. For whatever reason, God gave me that gift. I never asked for it. I don't deserve it. I enjoy it tremendously, but it came with a clear set of orders. God says to each leader what he says to me, "You lead as diligently as you possibly can. You maximize every ounce of leadership potential I put in you. Read. Study. Find a mentor. For the sake of the church and the world, develop this gift to the zenith of its potential in your life."

WAS JESUS LAISSEZ-FAIRE?

SOUND A BIT INTENSE? If you think it does, let's take a look at how Jesus, the ultimate leader, took his leadership challenge. When he was only twelve years old he told his parents, "I must be about my father's business." In other words: "Let the other kids play Nintendo and read comic books. I've got a world to change. And it's serious business." I'm fascinated by the very fact that he called it a *business*.

Years later, when he formally launched his ministry, he had a clear vision. He had a three-year strategic plan that included the selection and development of twelve disciples. He had a well-planned evangelism strategy that moved from concentric circles outward: first Jerusalem, then Judea, then Samaria, then the outermost parts of the earth. Jesus gave specific assignments to his followers, job descriptions, you might say. When his followers did their jobs well, he commended them, praised them, rewarded them. When they didn't, he confronted them and showed them how to do it right. Then he sent them out to do it again, but better this time.

Jesus was not the least bit laissez-faire about building the kingdom. His passion for the lost and his love for the church were so strong that he took his Father's business all the way to the cross. And I don't think Jesus is any more laissez-faire today than he was when he walked this earth in human flesh. I think he expects today's church leaders to put their best efforts into building prevailing churches. Of course he said we would not have to do this alone. He promised to gift us, empower us, and walk beside us. But we like Jesus, the greatest spiritual leader who ever walked the earth, need to be serious about "our Father's business." We need to remember that doing that requires prayer, spiritual discipline, dependence on the Holy Spirit—*and best leadership practices.* It's a both/and deal. We also need to accept that we will probably have to pay a price for devoting our lives to building the kingdom of God. Jesus did.

Can I come right out and say it? It's time for church leaders to *really lead.* It's time for us to be about our Father's business with diligence, dependence, and get-it-done leadership.

CHAPTER FOUR

Building a Kingdom Dream Team

Communities Close to a Leader's Heart

It WAS THE KIND OF PHONE CALL YOU NEVER FORGET. "HE'S GONE," a voice whispered on the other end of the line. "We know your schedule and the distance involved, so no one expects you to come to the funeral, but we thought you should know."

Immediately I dialed the number of my assistant, Jean, who worked her scheduling magic, and two days later my wife, Lynne, and I were standing by the young widow of one of Willow Creek's earliest staff members.

Tom was only in his forties, but leukemia had ravaged his body and taken his life. Now I was searching for a way to comfort his grief-stricken family. But before I could find the comforting words, his wife embraced me and quietly said, "Bill, you know Tom was never more alive than when he was a team member at Willow Creek. Those were the finest years of his life."

After the funeral service, Tom's brother pulled me off to the side and expressed similar thoughts. "I've never met you, but I just want you to know that from a brother's perspective Tom's years on the staff at your church were the best years of his life. I never knew him to be happier. I never knew him to be more excited or fulfilled than when he was on the team at Willow."

Then he grabbed my arm and choked out these words, "Tom was the only brother I ever had. Thanks for including him. Thanks for loving him and challenging him. Thanks for giving him a place to belong."

On the way home, I stared out the side window of the airplane and realized afresh what a privilege it is to be part of a loving, unified, energized team. I was so glad that Tom had been able to experience that. I remembered back to the years when he had sat around a table at Willow, sharing ideas, helping to form plans, giving and receiving energy in the powerful dynamic of a healthy team. How many people, I wondered, go to their graves without ever having experienced that? How many church leaders, pastors, devoted lay workers serve for years without ever being part of that?

For most of his life, my twenty-three-year-old son, Todd, has heard me teach and preach about community. And he's watched me lead and serve on many different teams around the church. But he had to experience it himself in order to understand why I am so passionate about it. The year he left for college in Southern California he started attending a Willow Creek Association church not far from his university. Within a few months Todd became involved in the leadership team of the youth ministry there.

Late one night when he was home for spring break, he climbed the stairs to my study and said, "Dad, I understand team community now. I understand that it's more than just working with other people, it's doing life *deeply* with one another as we serve together. And there's a huge difference between the two."

My spirit soared as I heard those words from my son. If only more leaders understood the distinction between "just working with other people" and "doing life deeply with one another as we serve together." Practicing the latter approach could improve the relational temperature of every church leadership circle in the world.

THREE EXAMPLES OF TEAM COMMUNITIES

SEVERAL YEARS AGO, I was invited to Washington, D.C., to attend the ceremony where Dr. Billy Graham would receive the Congressional Gold Medal of Honor. The Capitol Rotunda was filled with scores of government officials and dozens of world leaders. The ceremony was patriotic, stately, and very honoring. When Dr. Graham stood to receive his medal, he looked at the award and then said quietly, "This medal is really not for me. This medal is for our team. We've been together for forty-five years. Without each member my life would not have been the same. I owe them so much." Then he listed, one by one, the names of those who had formed the core of his evangelistic ministry. As he spoke their names he struggled to contain his emotion.

Still, I did not fully realize how deeply Dr. Graham and his associates valued team until, sometime later, I enjoyed a visit with him at his home in Montreat, North Carolina. He led me down the hill from his home and pointed out the houses being built nearby by some of his team members. Apparently, forty-five years of togetherness was not enough for this tightly knit team. Even as they neared the end of their lives, they wanted to be together, caring for and supporting each other, just as they had throughout their ministry years. I was deeply moved by their commitment to stay together all the way to the end.

Jesus too provides us a model of a leader who built a cohesive, loving team. One incident toward the end of his life is particularly touching. On the eve of his betrayal, he gathered his team together in the Upper Room and drew them close with these words: "I earnestly desire to share this meal with you." Then he broke the bread and shared the wine. His instructions for the future were specific. They were to continue this practice of remembering him, *in community*. Think of it. The first time communion was ever taken it was a team experience. And it's supposed to continue to be a team experience.

I count myself extremely fortunate to participate in several close ministry teams at Willow Creek Community Church. Many of us have been together nonstop for almost thirty years (counting the youth-ministry days that preceded Willow). Together we have experienced the highs and lows that weld hearts together.

The night after Willow's twentieth-anniversary celebration, I found a way to show these people just how much I treasure them. Through the generosity of a friend, I was able to whisk four of the church's founding couples to a Caribbean island for seven days. After swimming, sailing, and beach walking everyday, we spent the evenings gathered around a large table, sharing dinner and reminiscing about our lives together.

No one will ever forget those evenings. We laughed. We cried. Every meal stretched late into the night while we told stories and shared memories. On the last evening someone said, "I just want you all to know that I want to grow old with you! So don't anybody keel over or quit. Someday I want us to all be on a porch together, rocking and drinking and drooling until God takes us home. I want to die with this team."

As I drifted off to sleep that night I thought, "This is as good as it gets!"

Having just turned fifty, I have recently spent a lot of time thinking about what is essential to me. I realize that there are really only two things, besides my family, that really matter to me. First, I want to do God's bidding for the rest of my life. That's primary. But in addition to that, I want to do God's bidding in authentic community with people I love and who love me.

When these two essentials are realities, I have "life in all its fullness." Carrying people in my heart while we minister together, and being carried in their hearts as well, is what it means to be on a "dream team." It's almost like enjoying a bit of heaven on earth.

NO LEADER SHOULD MISS THIS

BUT EVEN WHILE I write this I feel a sense of sadness. Why? Because I'm keenly aware that many leaders have never experienced the richness of ministry life I'm describing, not when they were laypersons, not when they signed up to become a church staff member, not even after they became a senior leader.

What a loss to never know the mystery of a God-given solution coming to a ministry team that's been stuck, confused, and totally discouraged over a seemingly insurmountable obstacle. What a loss to never hear a timid team member say with Spirit-prompted boldness, "I know this sounds like a crazy idea, but what if we ..." What a loss to never look around the circle as eyes light up, bodies lean forward, and a team member says, "That's a fantastic idea!"

And then, what a terrible loss to miss what happens when the seed of an idea that has been watered with input from the team finally blossoms into a perfect ministry plan. How sad to miss the future shared moment when team members look back with amazement and someone says, "Do you remember when God broke through? Do you remember when that idea was born? Can you believe all that happened since then? Can you believe that we got to do this together?"

Those are holy moments, moments that bring you to your knees in thanksgiving for what God has done through the ragtag team of which you are a part. No leader should miss those kinds of moments.

A few years ago one of our WCA teams traveled to Germany to serve and train pastors. For months before we arrived, our German WCA team worked tirelessly to promote the conference. The response was so overwhelming that instead of doing one conference we ended up doing two conferences back-to-back.

To do a single three-day conference in a foreign country where every word must be communicated through translators and every team is jetlagged into near-senselessness is a huge challenge in itself. But that year, as soon as the first conference ended, we had to move the sound and lighting equipment to another venue so that three hours later we could start the second three-day conference. It was grueling to say the least.

Toward the end of the second conference we were utterly exhausted. Each message became a greater challenge to give and each song a greater challenge to sing. So when the team huddled together before and after each session, we did our best to cheer each other on and pump each other up. Then, during one of the final sessions, our vocal team sang an old hymn:

> The love of God is greater far
> Than tongue or pen can ever tell,
> It goes beyond the highest star
> And reaches to the lowest hell;
> The guilty pair, bowed down with care,
> God gave His Son to win:
> His erring child He reconciled
> And Pardoned from his sin.
>
> Could we with ink the ocean fill
> And were the skies of parchment made,
> Were every stalk on earth a quill
> And every man a scribe by trade,
> To write the love of God above
> Would drain the ocean dry,
> Nor could the scroll contain the whole
> Though stretched from sky to sky.
>
> O Love of God, how rich and pure!
> How measureless and strong!
> It shall forevermore endure
> The saints' and angel's song.[1]

---

[1] "The Love of God," F. M. Lehman, copyright 1917, renewed 1945 by Nazarene Publishing House.

On the last chorus, each vocalist dug down deep, summoning a final reserve of strength. To use an athletic expression, they left it all out on the field. When they finished, the place was paralyzed. No one applauded. No one moved. No one talked. Thirty-five hundred of us sat in stunned silence, awestruck by the love of God.

Finally I walked to the podium and dismissed the crowd. As people quietly exited, I went to find a space where I could be alone with God. I stood in the corner of an empty backstage room with my head down, my heart overwhelmed with the power and greatness of God. Several minutes passed like that, but then I realized I was not alone. The team had huddled around me with their heads bowed. When we lifted our heads and looked at each other, it was obvious we were all thinking the same thing: "This is as good as it gets—being powerfully used by God—*together*." Many of us in that circle had been ministering together for twenty years. We knew that not one of us could have experienced the moment we had just shared alone. Only together, working as a team under the inspiration and power of God, could we have enjoyed that remarkable experience.

That is one of the richest memories of my life, and I've had more of those experiences than I can count.

How I yearn for every church leader to enjoy holy team moments like that. Such experiences make church work sweet even during stressful times. It's what it means to live out the dream of Jesus, who prayed in his High Priestly prayer, "Oh God, may my followers become one."

DEFINE THE PURPOSE OF THE TEAM

I WOULD BE CRUEL to wave this kind of ministry oneness in front of other leaders if I were not strongly convinced that every leader is capable of building his or her own kingdom dream team. Really. Through the power of the Holy Spirit, the ability to build such a team is a standard component in a leader's gift package.

The first step in building a dream team is to define the purpose of the team. And I mean, define it with ruthless specificity. Forgive me for stating something so obvious, but sometimes it's the most obvious things that we miss.

When I first decided to put together a sailboat racing team, a guy who was helping me asked me a very important question. "Are you planning to race recreationally, or do you want to race at a competitive level? Are you just aiming to win local regattas or would you like to go all the way to the top and try to win a national championship? I ask you this because if you want to race recreationally, you can put together a team with Aunt Ethel, Cousin Eddie, and Buddy the Bartender. But if you want to race at the highest level of competition, you need to find some serious sailors."

He forced me to define the purpose of the team more specifically so I would know what kind of people to look for.

Now whenever pastors tell me they're going to put together a leadership team my reflex is to ask a few clarifying questions: "What *kind* of leadership team? What will be its purpose? Will it be to help you with your preaching? To create church policy? To discipline wayward church members? To buy property and build buildings?" I ask these questions because I know that these widely different tasks may well require people with widely different gifts, skills, and expertise. Leaders must be painfully specific about the nature and purpose of the team. What do we want this particular team to accomplish?

THE "THREE Cs" OF TEAM SELECTION

THE NEXT STEP IN building a dream team is to establish clear criterion for the selection of specific team members. What kind of person is needed to fill each particular position on the team? We need to look for certain characteristics and qualities in order of their importance.

When John Wooden, the legendary UCLA basketball coach, was asked what top three traits he looked for in prospective team members, he answered simply: Talent. Talent. Talent. (In that order.) While Wooden's criterion may have been appropriate for building a basketball team, I believe there is far more to consider when assembling a kingdom dream team.

Let me share what I look for in prospective team members at Willow Creek Community Church and at the Willow Creek Association. My selection process is based on "three Cs": first character, then competence, and finally chemistry with me and with the rest of the team. Character. Competence. Chemistry. After experimenting with different selection criteria through the years, I have landed on these three in the precise order in which they are mentioned.

When searching for someone to add to a volunteer team or a paid staff position, I remind myself, *Character first.* By this I mean that I need to have confidence in a person's walk with Jesus Christ. I need to know that they are committed to spiritual disciplines. I need to see evidence of honesty, teachability, humility, reliability, a healthy work ethic, and a willingness to be entreated.

I didn't always place character above competence, but I do now. I have learned that in church work an occasional lapse in competence can be accepted. But lapses in character create problems with far-reaching implications. A breakdown in character tends to breed distrust and alienate team members. It also de-motivates the leader when it comes to investing time and emotional energy into that particular team member. And of course, if the leader does not deal with the wayward team member wisely, he or she may lose the respect of other team members.

A different leader might rank team selection criteria in another way, but for me it's character first. Another sailing story may help to illustrate why.

One season we were short a crewmember so we invited a new sailor to join our team. His competence was off the chart, but over time, his character became an issue. First, he was arrogant. When he met someone, his standard introductory line was, "My name is Don. The women call me Dangerous Don." I thought our regular crewmembers were going to hang over the side and puke when they first heard that.

Over time we noticed that Don frequently fudged with the truth. Then he consistently began showing up late for practice, never offering an apology or acknowledging that he might have inconvenienced others. When small items started disappearing from the boat, I knew there was serious trouble brewing. The other guys started locking their wallets in their cars instead of leaving them in the top drawer of the galley as we had always done. Finally, I had to pull the plug. Dangerous Don was a tremendous sailor, but his character didn't cut the mustard.

For me, church work is no different from sailing when it comes to the issue of character. I used to think that if I discovered a potential team member who was terrifically competent but a little shaky in regard to character, I could go with the competence and address the character defects over time. Ever the optimist, I thought that if that person were in a healthy church environment, surrounded by godly people who would hold him or her accountable, it would eventually work out.

But after thirty years of optimism I have had to admit defeat. Face it. Every adult interviewing for a key role has already spent twenty-five, thirty, thirty-five years in a process of character formation. Not much is going to change after that. So I look for character that has already been positively formed. (Obviously, when discipling a new Christian we need to realize that it will take time for that person's character to conform to the image of Christ. But that's another matter entirely; when we're talking about forming a leadership dream team, we are most likely not talking about new Christians.)

So during the selection process I work very hard to discern a candidate's character. I check references. I speak at length with people who know the person well. I'm looking for any red flags pursuant to issues of character. Better for me to catch inconsistencies now than force a whole team to catch them later.

What do I do if an existing team member begins to display lapses in character? I act as soon as I'm aware of a problem. I talk with the individual immediately, hoping that together we can discern the root causes of the problem. Then I ask him or her to face it, confess it, and make changes with God's help. Often I will also suggest Christian counseling.

But if there is a continuing pattern of inconsistency, I usually ask the person to leave the team. I know that may seem extreme, but I've learned that it is nearly impossible for a team to fulfill its purpose when one member is involved in the difficult work of character reclamation.

When someone is asked to leave a team, our elders put together a spiritual restoration plan, offer financial assistance, and recommend continued Christian counseling. We truly want to see the person's character transformed through the work of God, but we have learned that significant character change rarely happens if the person remains in their staff or volunteer position. In my early days of leadership, I was extremely patient in regard to slips of character, hoping against hope that "things would just get better." Now I know that usually doesn't happen. The leader must take action—the sooner, the better.

AFTER CHARACTER COMES COMPETENCE

MY SECOND SELECTION CRITERION is competence. And I don't apologize for shooting high. I look for the highest level of competence I can find. I ask God to help me find someone whose spiritual gifts have been developed and refined over many years. If we're looking for someone to join our teaching team, I ask God to help us find a person with extremely strong teaching gifts, certainly someone more gifted as a teacher than I am. Several years ago when we added a new midweek teacher, I was thrilled to discover that he was an even more phenomenal teacher than I had expected. I still thank God for sending John Ortberg to us.

If I'm looking for a Director of Operations, I look for someone with monster administrative gifts and a stellar track record of performance. Years ago I realized that if I didn't start surrounding myself with some really outstanding people I would be overwhelmed by the challenges of leading Willow. Now when I look around the table during our management team meetings I see a Harvard MBA, a Stanford MBA, one Ph.D., two individuals with law degrees, and several with master's degrees. I am the only one seriously lacking in credentials!

Peter Drucker, the best-selling management author, once told me that the team members I was looking for at that time were most likely neither unhappy nor unemployed. "If you find someone whose qualifications look good, but he or she is unhappy or unemployed, be very cautious. The kind of people you are looking for are probably making huge contributions and setting records somewhere. They are probably deliriously happy and much loved by the people they work with. Go after that type. Go after proven competence."

That was very valuable counsel that I follow to this day. It echoes the words of the apostle Paul who insists in 1 Timothy 3:10 that every new deacon should be "first tested."

So first look for excellent character, and then shoot for the moon when it comes to competence.

THE THIRD "C" IS CHEMISTRY

THE THIRD "C" I look for is chemistry, a relational fit with me as well as with other team members. Ken Blanchard, coauthor of *The One-Minute Manager,* counseled me never to invite a person onto my team who doesn't have a positive emotional effect on me the minute he or she walks into my office.

I initially thought that counsel was a bit extreme. "Come on, Ken," I challenged him, "I'm not looking for a golfing buddy. I just need a capable person to work faithfully in our church." That was many years ago. Today I am a convert to the doctrine of chemistry. Why? Because so much of my time (except when I'm preparing sermons) is spent in team. Nearly every moment of my working day I'm sitting around a table with the elder team, the board of directors, the management team, the teaching team, the programming team, the WCA leadership team, or the international conference team. For hundreds of hours each year, I sit in small circles working on kingdom challenges with other people. I don't know how to say this diplomatically, but it helps if I really like being with those people! So if two job candidates have equal character and competence, I'll give the nod to the person whose personality and temperament blends with the other team members and with me.

I admit this without a hint of apology. One of the reasons I am having such a ball doing ministry these days is that finally, after almost three decades of team-building, all our major leadership teams are built according to the criteria I've been describing. Throughout our teams we have people with sky-high character, off-the-chart competence, and extraordinary chemistry. What's not to like? When I go to work each day I feel like a schoolboy going out for recess.

But let me remind you again that it's taken me thirty years to get to this point. So if you lead a church that is four years old and you don't have a kingdom dream team yet, don't despair. "Stay the course," would be my advice, "but keep the selection bar high."

DON'T OVERLOOK YOUR OWN PEOPLE

OCCASIONALLY I'M ASKED WHERE I find such great people to hire. My answer might be surprising. Almost seventy-five percent of our leaders have come right out of Willow. These are people who have proven their character, competence, and chemistry fit while serving in volunteer positions within our ministry.

While developing our own leaders from within has proven to be our best way to form dream teams, there are times that we, like most other churches, need to look beyond our walls for key staff. We have discovered that one of the benefits of being a member of the Willow Creek Association is the networking opportunity it affords. When church leaders gather together at conferences they are constantly rubbing shoulders with, or hearing about, potential staff members who share their vision and values.

Our experience has been that even when we hire very carefully from outside, our batting average is less than fifty percent when it comes to creating an ideal, long-term working relationship. But when we hire from inside Willow or the WCA, that percentage jumps dramatically. The lesson is obvious: hire from within whenever you can.

TO BUILD PERFORMANCE, START WITH THE LEADER

ONCE A LEADER DEFINES the purpose of a team and recruits team members, then he or she must ask the really big questions: What will it take for this team to reach its full potential? What kind of leader do I need to be for this to happen?

I've never been impressed with the advice of those who suggest that teams can be self-directed or led by rotating leaders. I side strongly with those who believe that the most crucial factor in a team's performance is the effectiveness of its clearly defined leader.

Each team needs a top quality leader who will:

Keep the team focused on the mission
Make sure the right people with the right gifts and right
    talents are in the right positions
Maximize every team member's contribution
Evenly distribute the load so that morale stays high and
    burnout stays low

Facilitate communication so that all team members remain
in the information loop

Assess and raise the level of community within the team.

These are huge challenges. I think it's extremely naïve to think
that teams can flourish without a focused leader pouring time and
energy into achieving these goals.

TO BUILD COMMUNITY, USE COMMUNITY EXERCISES

SPEAKING OF NAÏVE, early in my ministry I assumed that community
"just happened," that if team members spent enough time working
together, they would inevitably develop meaningful, supportive
relationships. I discovered years ago, however, that a deep sense of
camaraderie and unity rarely develops spontaneously. In fact, one
of the most important roles a leader plays is to guide team members
into a deeper experience of community.

One effective way to do this is to use community-enhancing
exercises. For what it's worth, let me share some specific exercises
that I and others have used to encourage deeper relating patterns in
Willow teams.

The Hot Seat

Several years ago I took a staff team of fifteen members to our
church camp in the Upper Peninsula of Michigan. Every afternoon
we sat in a circle on a deck overlooking a beautiful river. In the middle of the circle we placed a chair that we called "the hot seat."
One by one, we each took the hot seat and had to answer a series
of questions posed by other team members:

What was your greatest disappointment in the first third
of your life? The second third? Recently?

Who has been the most outrageously loving person in
your life?

What was the greatest achievement you experienced before
the tenth grade?

We made sure to inject some pure curiosity questions:

What would you do if you won the lottery?
Where would you spend a three-week vacation if money
    were no object?
Of all living people, who would you most want to have a
    three-hour dinner with and why?

Several of our hot seat sessions lasted for three or four hours. Some of the answers will be remembered for years. I agree with whoever said, "Knowing leads to loving." It is impossible to listen to the heartfelt reflections of a team member without being drawn into a deeper relationship with that person.

What Do You Want on Your Tombstone?

More recently, on a management team retreat, I gave each team member a sheet of construction paper with a tombstone drawn on it. Then, one by one, I asked team members to leave the room while the rest of us worked together to write an epitaph for the person waiting outside.

Our goal was to capture the essence of the team member on whom we were focusing. When we agreed on an appropriate epitaph, we wrote our words very neatly on that person's tombstone. Then we invited him or her back into the room and said, "Of course, we hope you don't die soon, but if you did, here's what we would remember about you." We read the person's epitaph aloud, and team members added personal comments. The love and emotion in the room was palpable.

When the retreat ended, I collected the tombstones and started walking toward the dumpster. The team was horrified. One person suggested that we get them framed so we could hang them in our respective offices. I thought he was joking, but in the end, that's what we all did. Visit Willow and you'll see them proudly displayed.

Whenever we walk into each other's offices and see the tombstones we are reminded of that extraordinary afternoon.

Chagall Would Have Loved This

At another retreat Greg Hawkins, our executive pastor, led us in an exercise that proved to be a stretch for those of us on the management team who are artistically challenged. He asked us to paint a picture about the condition of our souls. Can you imagine someone like me describing the condition of my soul with a paintbrush?

But we all did it. Afterwards, we sat around a crackling fire and explained the meaning of our paintings. Some were vibrant and colorful, others were a little dark. Someone said, "Obviously, according to my picture, I'm not doing very well right now. This is a very difficult time in my life." That opened a door for us to hear what was troubling this team member. And that is precisely what all these exercises are intended to do: to create open doors for knowing and being known.

Take Up the Basin and Towel

Years ago our programming director, Nancy Beach, led a particularly moving exercise with her team of artists. After reading John 13, the passage about Jesus washing the feet of his disciples, Nancy and her team actually took basins of water and small towels and bathed each other's feet. I heard from a number of those team members that it was one of the most powerful team experiences they had ever had.

Community building exercises such as these have never been easy for me to plan or to participate in. I always have to fight my temptation to "just get to work," but I do them because I have discovered the benefits of working in true community. It's not enough for leaders to try to improve the performance of teams. We have the equally important responsibility to be consistent community builders. I hope every senior leader reading these words will take this responsibility seriously.

BUILD TEAM PERFORMANCE BY ESTABLISHING CLEAR GOALS

I MENTIONED EARLIER THAT I'm a major advocate of establishing BHAGs—big, hairy, audacious goals. But goals have to be more than big. They also have to be clear. The old saying is true: What gets measured, gets done. Without clear goals, most teams flounder. They waste time, lose energy, get distracted, and eventually become demoralized.

Jesus, just before he ascended into heaven, said, according to my translation of Matthew 28:19–20, "Okay team, here's the goal: Go into all the world and preach the gospel. Lead every man, woman, and child to faith. Then grow them up by teaching them to observe all I have commanded you. Ready. Set. Go." And they did.

Part of the reason Jesus' disciples turned the world upside down is that they had been commissioned by the world's greatest leader with the clearest, most exciting goal ever set: world redemption through the ministry of the church.

Church leaders must do what Jesus did. We must sit down with teams all across the church and establish clear, challenging, God-honoring goals. Then we need to inspire team members to roll up their sleeves and get creative. We need to challenge them to fast, to pray, to pull together, and to give their best efforts in order to achieve the goals for the glory of the One whose name we bear.

As we've learned to do this at Willow, we've seen tremendous power unleashed. Recently Nancy Beach commissioned her programming department with this goal: Create a moving, colorful, powerful outreach event, an artistically excellent presentation through which the gospel can be communicated to large numbers of unchurched people in our community.

Under her leadership and challenged by that clear goal, her team created one of the most innovative evangelistic events our church has ever offered to our community. We filled our auditorium ten times with thousands of people who heard the truth about Jesus Christ. But it all started with the assignment of a clear goal.

I never tire of watching teams rise to the challenge of reaching a God-honoring goal. Yes, it takes extraordinary leadership energy to set appropriate goals, to align people to them, and to inspire team members to reach them. But let me remind you, the payoff is huge. And eternal.

BUILD TEAM PERFORMANCE BY REWARDING ACHIEVEMENT

FINALLY, A LEADER MUST reward teams for work well done. Some church leaders are squeamish about rewarding those who work effectively. But Jesus was not vague about the concept of rewards. He often promised devoted followers great reward "in this life and the next."

The apostle Paul often heaped praise and recognition on those who worked diligently in the local church. He sometimes ended his epistles with the names of people he wanted to honor. Apparently he thought it was important to publicly acknowledge the efforts of people who had worked hard for the cause. He even stated that certain people should receive double honor because of their faithful performance.

At Willow, we often acknowledge the extraordinary effort of staff members by paraphrasing the words of the apostle Paul in Philippians 2:29. In that text Paul exhorts the church leaders at Philippi to hold certain church members in "high regard." So when we want to acknowledge the outstanding efforts of an individual or a team, we often stand them in front of the whole staff or church and shout in unison, "WE HOLD YOU IN HIGH REGARD! WAY TO GO!" Then we cheer wildly.

If you doubt the effectiveness of this approach, I simply invite you to try it sometime.

We also believe it's important to recognize and reward the efforts of the thousands of volunteers serving Christ at Willow. They form the backbone of our ministry. They are the unseen heroes who work so diligently to keep our ministry functioning and growing. Our paid staff knows that we would be in major trouble without them. So, many years ago we decided to acknowledge their contribution with an Annual Volunteer Appreciation evening at our midweek services.

You have to see this to believe it. Each year we literally roll out red carpets at all the major entrances to our buildings. Balloons line both sides of the red carpet, and staff people are stationed at all the doors.

When the volunteers get out of their cars, they walk the red carpets and are cheered on by the Willow Creek staff. "Yea, you! We're so glad you are on the team! Way to go!"

All that happens before they even enter the building.

Once inside they see the balloons and decorations that the staff put up in their honor. The whole service is a celebration of volunteerism in our church. I do my best to preach a message that heaps honor on each and every volunteer.

After the service we invite everybody to a lively reception that includes food, music, and other festivities. If you are thinking this sounds like a lot of time and money, you are right. But again, the payoff is huge. Ask any Willow volunteer.

As I said at the beginning of this chapter, at this point in my life, I only want two things: to do God's bidding and to do it with people I love.

A few months ago a group of my teammates threw a fiftieth birthday party for me. Of course, it included the typical good-natured bashing about growing older. But there were holy moments that night as well, as we shared the memories of almost three decades together. That night as I drifted off to sleep, I thought to myself, *I am the richest man in the world! I have what many leaders only dream about: A clear calling from God that still makes my heart race each day, and a team of the most remarkable people I've ever met to share the adventure with me.*

Tell me leaders, what beats that?

CHAPTER FIVE

The Resource Challenge

The Test of a Leader's Mettle

O F ALL THE CHALLENGES OF LEADERSHIP, THE ONE I WAS LEAST PRE-pared for is what I have come to call "The Resource Challenge." I was to learn the hard way that unless I was willing to become the CRR (chief resource raiser) our new church would be short lived. It would starve to death from lack of funding.

During my three years in youth ministry, I learned many of the classic functions of leadership—vision casting, team building, problem solving, and goal setting—but because we were a sub-ministry of an affluent church I never had to worry about resources. The church covered our financial needs. It provided us with facili-ties and equipment at no cost, a generous budget to cover ministry expenses, and a salary that took care of my personal needs.

But when we left that church to start Willow Creek Commu-nity Church, all of that changed dramatically. Literally overnight I was forced to face a harsh reality: We had no facilities, no equip-ment, no ministry budgets, and no salaries. Worse yet, there was no one to complain to. We had no people! My romance with the notion of *building* an Acts 2 church had blinded me to the harsh realities of *funding* one.

Complicating matters was the fact that we had already announced the starting date for our new church. We had passed out invitations and flyers that publicized our meeting place at the Willow Creek Theater in Palatine. We had formed music and ministry teams. We had leased our staff offices.

It took me about five minutes to realize that we needed a massive infusion of money and we needed it fast.

Fighting off an old-fashioned panic attack, I came up with a plan. Back then I knew of just one sure way to make money. So taking a cue from my days at our family's produce business, I ordered twelve hundred cases of tomatoes. Then, on a Saturday in August of 1975, I challenged the group of high school kids who formed the core of our start-up team to sell tomatoes door-to-door. Unfortunately I had failed to notice the backyard gardens filled with tomato plants that dotted our community; by the end of the day we were selling our tomatoes for twenty-five cents per basket. Still, we raised several thousand dollars and solved our financial problems.

For about a week.

I remember going to bed thinking, *We can't sell tomatoes every Saturday, and I don't think this resource challenge is going to go away. I had better figure out what it really means to be a CRR.*

MONEY MEMORIES

MOST OF MY MINISTRY memories of the late seventies have to do with trying to deal with Willow's lack of resources. One of my early cohorts was a music guy named Dave Holmbo. Not only was Dave a creative genius, but he also had a monster work ethic. He often put in eighty-hour weeks, diligently transcribing music scores by copying vocal arrangements and orchestra parts by hand. One day, without telling me, he ordered some special pencils that musicians use for this purpose. When the unexpected bill for $19.00 worth of those pencils landed on my desk, I walked into Dave's office and said, "Dave, you're killing us. We can't afford pencils like that. You've got to find another way to write your arrangements."

These days musicians at Willow have the latest computers to help them do their work, but back then we lived so close to the financial edge that $19.00 was a very big deal.

I had a similar financial confrontation with our production volunteers. Because we didn't have our own facility and couldn't find a rental facility where we could schedule all our events, we were constantly moving from place to place. Each time we moved—from the Willow Creek Theater, to various high school auditoriums and cafeterias, and even to the local Elks Club—we had to set up and tear down sound and lighting equipment. In each place, after all the equipment was in place, the volunteers had to tape down all the electrical cords with gray duct tape so that people wouldn't trip over them. Because we did so many set-ups and tear-downs the production people started ordering duct tape by the case, again, without telling me.

After one particular weekend when we had received a very low offering, the financial pressures became almost more than I could bear. With that problem weighing heavily on me, I walked into the rented building we were using for our midweek service and noticed how liberally the volunteer stage crew was applying the tape. *Don't they know how much that tape costs?*

I snapped.

I called the volunteers together and let them have it. "Guys, you are wasting very expensive tape and the church has no money. You don't need a full width of tape to attach a single cord to the floor. New rule: From here on out, I'm asking everyone to tear the tape in half, like this . . ." Then I demonstrated my cost-saving idea in front of them as dramatically as possible.

I can still remember their shocked expressions. Someone managed to mutter back, "Okay, okay," but they must have thought I had lost my mind.

Here's another snapshot of those years: The only office space we could afford to rent had bare cement floors. If we wanted carpet we would have to purchase it ourselves. So we did, ordering the cheapest stuff we could find. When I placed the order I warned the storeowner that we would probably not be able to pay him all at once.

He was gracious and said, "Well, you're a church. I trust you. I know you're going to be good for it. Pay me what you can when you can."

About a month later the bill arrived. I remember the exact amount. It was $973.00. Since we didn't have *any* money at that moment I put the bill on a stack of other unpaid bills. When the storeowner called me several weeks later to request payment, I reminded him that he had agreed to an installment plan.

"Yes, that's true," he responded, "but could you send me *something?*"

"I will right now," I told him. I reached into the top drawer of my desk and wrote out a check for $5.00 and put it in the mail.

When he got the check, he called me immediately and asked, "What's this? Are you kidding?"

"No," I responded, embarrassed, "but I'm promising you. I'll send you five bucks every week."

And I did. I sent him $5.00 a week until we paid off the whole thing. Almost three decades later I still get a knot in my stomach when I drive past that carpet store.

PUSHED TO THE BREAKING POINT

ONE THING THAT COMPLICATED our resource challenge was that we started Willow with high school and college students. Few of us had fulltime jobs, so we had plenty of time and energy to offer, but no money. I knew that if we didn't start attracting some bona fide adults who had reasonable incomes, we were going to go bankrupt. So I started praying fervently about this.

One Sunday a guy who appeared to be a businessman—an

actual adult who looked like he had a real job—walked into one of our services. The guy looked normal. His suit fit (none of us even had suits). My hopes went sky high.

After church we talked a little and then he said, "Hey, I really like this church. Can I take you out to lunch this week?"

"Sure," I responded without hesitation, certain that my prayers had been answered.

A few days later he picked me up for lunch in a twenty-eight-foot-long silver Cadillac. He took me to a very expensive restaurant and casually told me to order anything I wanted. At twenty-three years of age I had no pride. I ordered huge.

Halfway through lunch he started asking questions about the church. "I really like your new church," he finally said as dessert arrived. "Could I be of any help?"

That's all the opening I needed. "Oh man," I said, "you could help in all kinds of ways!"

Then he asked more directly, "What's your biggest need?"

"Well," I answered, "I know you're new, and you probably don't want to hear about our problems, but we're on the edge financially. I mean, we're a week away from financial extinction every single week. None of us earn salaries. We've already given up our life's savings. I don't know how many more weeks we can keep the doors open."

To my great relief he responded with a confident smile and said, "I think I can help you with that problem. I've never given anything to any church, but I like your church so you can expect a gift from me this week. I'll send it in the mail."

That next week I lived every day in great anticipation. Each morning I ran to the mailbox hoping for his letter. Finally near the end of the week, it arrived. *Here it is,* I thought. *Our ship has come in!* Eagerly I tore open that envelope . . . and discovered a check for ten bucks! I almost passed out. For days I had to fight off carnal thoughts about sabotaging his silver Cadillac. The resource challenge was pushing me to the breaking point.

A STEEP AND NECESSARY LEARNING CURVE

I WAS QUICKLY FORCED to come to grips with the fact that from a human perspective the point leader stands accountable for raising and allocating funds for the entire organization. The point leader has to raise money for the staff, for the ministry programs, and for his or her family as well.

For those unprepared to be a fundraiser, as most pastors are, that is a daunting reality.

Theologian R. C. Sproul once asked me how much ministry I thought I could do for a hundred bucks. I assumed he was hoping for some deep theological response, but before I could think of one he answered the question himself. "You can do about a hundred dollars' worth." He was simply making the point that a fruitful ministry requires resources.

Be as theological as you want to be, but the church will never reach her full redemptive potential until a river of financial resources starts flowing in her direction. And like it or not, it is the leader's job to create that river and to manage it wisely. The sooner a leader realizes that the better.

My goal in the rest of this chapter is to help leaders develop the skills required to become CRRs. I will start with some ground-level truths that every leader must understand to move into this role successfully.

RESOURCE TRUTH #1: GOD IS THE ULTIMATE RESOURCE SUPPLIER

AN OLD CHILDREN'S SONG describes God's resources quite graphically: "He owns the cattle on a thousand hills, the wealth in every mine." In Psalm 50:12 God himself echoes this theme when he says that "the world is mine, and all that is in it." God's resources, in other words, are unlimited.

Many church leaders fall into the trap of believing that some person in their church is their ultimate resource supplier. Not so. People are the conduits of God's supply, but they are not ultimately responsible for it. God alone controls the flow of the financial river we need.

Leaders also need to understand that God is not just *able* to help, he is actually *eager* to help. The church is his bride. It is his gift to the world. No one wants to see a church appropriately resourced more than God does.

I learned this lesson at a critical point in Willow's growth. Late in the 1970s we were in a huge building program for our original auditorium. In a radical act of faith, we had committed to 2 million dollars beyond our budget, a budget that had already stretched us to the limit. People had given virtually everything they had to give. Several hundred people, Lynne and I and most of the staff included, had even taken out bank loans to keep the project going.

Then the U.S. economy collapsed. Unemployment soared and interest rates rose to twenty-one percent. Just when I thought things could not get worse the largest donor in our church left. This was the man we had all been counting on to bail us out if everything went south. That's when I had to define, once and for all, the difference between the conduit and the ultimate source of supply.

Yes, it was a heavy blow to lose our largest donor. But I realized that just because he had left our church, that didn't mean God had left it. God had called us to start a church to reach lost people, and everything in my spirit told me he was still with us and still cheering us on. He was still the ultimate supplier. We just had to keep moving forward in faith.

I told nervous board members that God was still on the throne, that he still had plenty, and that he was probably already looking around for new conduits through which to send resources our way. Because most of the board had backed our bank loan with the equity in their homes, they had more than passing interest in exactly what God was "probably doing."

In the months following that crisis of faith, we had the privilege of seeing God work in a mighty way on our behalf. Not only did he pour his resources through new conduits, but eventually the large donor who had left came back. He has helped us financially and in many other ways ever since. Lessons like that one are not soon forgotten.

Leaders will sleep a lot better at night once they nail down this fundamental principle. The ultimate supplier for the resources we need is the God who wants to see his church built even more than we do. And he has plenty.

RESOURCE TRUTH #2: UNDER THE RIGHT CIRCUMSTANCES, PEOPLE LOVE TO GIVE

CRRs NEED TO START by assuming that people are predisposed to give. Think about it: the alternative assumption is that people are basically greedy and miserly and hate to give. Believing *that* will inevitably lead to destructive dynamics in a leader's approach to raising money. A leader who is convinced that his or her job is to wrench dollars from people who are adamantly opposed to parting with them cannot help but come up with a fundraising strategy that is manipulative and that produces guilt.

Such an approach hurts people and over time destroys churches. But fundraising doesn't have to be a negative experience for anyone involved. I firmly believe that if the right people are presented with the right kingdom opportunity in the right way at the right time, the result will be a joyful and generous outpouring of support. The whole world witnessed this principle in the aftermath of September 11. Billions of dollars were raised for the families of victims even though our country was in the midst of a frightening recession.

I've always tried to approach fundraising efforts in our church from a positive perspective that treats people with dignity. I define my goal like this: To offer wonderful people fantastic opportunities to invest in the kingdom, if God so leads them. Who can argue with an approach like that?

RESOURCE TRUTH #3: FUNDING MINISTRY PROVES THE CHARACTER OF A LEADER LIKE NO OTHER CHALLENGE

I WONDER HOW MANY leaders occasionally fantasize about someone like Bill Gates funneling a few billion from his piggy bank into their church account. That would be Nirvana, wouldn't it? The resource challenge would be met once and for all. The entire gift could be invested in an interest-bearing account and the church would be resourced permanently. This would enable the leader to get on with casting vision and building teams and it would let the congregation breathe a little easier too. People could focus on finding their spiritual gifts and serving without the hassle of stewardship campaigns and building fund drives.

Wouldn't that feel like heaven?

I'm not so sure. In fact, I'm quite certain that if Bill Gates were to offer to transfer a billion or two into Willow's coffers, I'd turn it down. (Okay, I might humbly accept a couple hundred million, but nothing with a "b" in front of it. I do have my scruples.)

The reason I'd refuse the gift is that I believe there are tremendous spiritual benefits associated with having to face financial challenges. Sometimes I get urgent requests from young pastors. They write: "Bill, we visited Willow and saw that your church is several hundred thousand dollars ahead of budget, and it's only midyear. How about writing us a check for a hundred grand? You guys wouldn't even miss it and it would relieve so much pressure around our church."

I receive hundreds of such requests and I answer them all the same way. "The very pressure that you're feeling right now is the stuff that God wants to use to move you and your people into higher levels of commitment and trust."

Then I expand the basis of my *no*. "I'm not trying to be hardhearted. I just want you to know that in the early days of this church nothing deepened my trust in the goodness, grace, and miracle-working power of God like the financial pressures that we faced every week, the very same kinds of pressures you are facing today. Don't underestimate the value of the spiritual growth that will take place in you and in your church as you address these resource challenges."

THE BENEFITS OF ENDURING TRYING TIMES

BY MOST STANDARDS, the home I grew up in would be considered affluent. But, when I left the family business my dad believed I should leave empty handed. And I did. So when Lynne and I started Willow, we had no money. The church couldn't afford to pay us a salary for almost three years, so I worked at night at the Water Street Produce Market in downtown Chicago and Lynne taught private flute lessons. We also took two boarders into our two-bedroom cracker-box home and made a highly sophisticated financial arrangement with them. Whenever any of us would earn some money, we would put a portion of it on top of the refrigerator. Every day we would pray that by the end of the month there would be enough money for us to pay the mortgage.

We did that for three years and never missed a mortgage payment.

We never missed a meal either, thanks to the anonymous friends who occasionally felt prompted by God to leave a bag of groceries on our front porch. Other people gave us used furniture without which our little house would have been virtually empty. Never before had I been in a totally dependent relationship with God in regards to money and daily necessities.

Once during this trying period a longtime friend who worked on a drill press for eight hours a day earning minimum wage gave me some money. His generosity touched me very deeply. For the first time I personally experienced the Acts 2 idea of interdependence in the family of God. Even more significantly, it melted my pride. This was a guy whose family had lived on the poor side of the Michigan town where I had grown up on the affluent side. Now I was the one needing help.

In those years of scarcity I found God to be utterly, wonderfully, and consistently faithful, the ultimate promise keeper. I don't think that conviction could have been forged in me in any other way. Scarcity can produce amazing spiritual fruit.

Almost three decades later I still draw on those early years of struggle when I teach on the trustworthiness of God. Those years made God's faithfulness more than theory to me.

During those challenging days the Willow congregation was learning these lessons right along with me. When we initially bought land and built buildings, we prayed together like we had never prayed before. We had home meetings. We fasted. Many of us cashed out completely. People sold condos, cars, jewelry. Our faith grew and we became bonded together like never before.

In February of 1981 we held the first service on our own property in our new auditorium. Before the service I invited the core members who had sacrificed so much and trusted God so completely to join together in the auditorium before we opened the doors to the rest of the congregation. I'll never forget that scene. Scores of believers were huddled in little groups with their arms around each other, bawling like babies. God had made the impossible possible. By his supernatural power he had moved the resource mountain. None of us would ever be the same again.

Several years ago at Willow's twentieth anniversary, we held a Founders' Dinner to honor the three hundred people who had helped us make that initial move from the theater onto our own campus. These were the people who had taken out the bank loans, sold their cars, and cancelled their vacations to fund our first building. That night I addressed the group. When I looked into their faces I was so overwhelmed by the memories of their radical generosity that I started to feel guilty. "I am really sorry," I said, "for asking you to make such unbelievable sacrifices during those early years."

Afterwards, several of the founders admonished me. "Don't ever apologize," they said, "for calling us to makes sacrifices for something that's come to mean so much to us. We walk around with the knowledge that God used us to provide a home for Willow Creek. It's like we've been given lifetime badges of honor."

Through the years, many of those resource heroes have been moved by their corporations to different parts of the country, but they are still attached to the Willow family. Whenever they hear of how God is using our church throughout the world they have the satisfaction of knowing that they played a significant role in making that happen, because they were one of the early conduits of God's resources.

Let me say it again. Nothing tests the mettle of church leaders and members more than the resource challenge. So rather than looking for quick fixes, lottery wins, or Bill Gates bailouts, leaders must willingly, courageously, and expectantly accept the resource challenge. We must allow the pressures of scarcity to teach us all we can learn about God, about our people, and about ourselves.

With those ground-level truths established, we can now move on. The following five principles of raising and allocating resources build upon the basic truths already mentioned. I am convinced, based on thirty years of personal experience and of observing other leaders, that those who practice these five principles will see a river of resources released for God's glory in the local church.

RESOURCES AND THE EDUCATION PRINCIPLE

IN THE VERY EARLY days of Willow Creek, an unchurched friend of mine crossed the line of faith and started attending church. After one of our services he asked me, "What's the deal with the offering basket?"

Not knowing where he was going with this I asked him what he meant. He said, "I have no clue how this whole thing works. Who is supposed to give, how often, and how much?"

His question helped me realize the importance of the Education Principle. Most leaders assume that everybody who comes to church knows God's mind on financial matters. But the truth is that many people are absolutely clueless regarding the basic principles of Christian financial management. Leaders and teachers need to educate their congregations before they can expect them to honor God with their money and eventually get excited about resourcing the church.

I strongly suggest that church leaders and teachers present a two- or three-week series on the biblical principles of money management every year. In the U.S., January is the ideal time for this because that's when most people are rethinking personal budgets. In other countries there may be a more appropriate time of the year for such a series.

In these stewardship series we need to explain that according to the Bible earning money is a good thing, while getting into excessive debt is a bad thing. We need to explain that Christ followers are called to live within their means, to give a minimum of ten percent of their earnings back to God's work in their local church, and to give sacrificially to the poor as the Spirit prompts them.

Both believers and seekers need to be reminded of the practices of biblical money management at least once a year. At Willow we go far beyond a single annual reminder. Each January, after our money management series, we offer a budget-planning workshop as a follow-up. Each year hundreds of people spend half a Saturday learning how to put together a God-honoring budget.

We also have a thriving sub-ministry called Good $ense that provides training and individual counsel for people who are trying to align their finances with biblical principles. Good $ense volunteers work year around and assist hundreds of people in our church.[1]

If you think about it, very few parents teach their kids the disciplines of money management these days, and few if any courses

---

[1]For more information about Good $ense, or to purchase the Good $ense Ministry kit, visit *www.GoodSenseMinistry.com.*

on this subject are offered in high schools and colleges. Where do we expect people to learn this important information?

If we need proof that money matters are out of control, all we need to do is look at debt statistics. Recent statistics show the average credit card debt in the U.S. is $8,300. One Saturday, after I'd taught about the dangers of credit card debt, a young man in his early thirties approached me in the bullpen. "I'm one of the people you talked about today," he said. "I maxed out my credit card and didn't even consider it a problem. But today I have decided to go home and cut up the card and begin making the minimum monthly payment until it's gone."

"How long do you think that will take?" I asked him.

"I don't know," he admitted. "My debt is pretty high, even a little higher than the national average you mentioned. But I'm committed. I'm going to stick with this plan all the way to the end."

The next day I ran the numbers for a debt of $8,300. If you paid the minimum payment on this debt of $8,300, it would take 34.5 years to pay it off. Interest would total $11,367.14, and the total amount paid would be $19,667.14. (Statistics from www.cardweb.com.)

Most people have no idea of the pain associated with financial mismanagement. If we leaders really love our people, we must educate and inspire them in the direction of financial freedom. It is unfair for us to expect people whose finances are the cause of pain or frustration to be conduits of God's resources.

If you are not sure how to approach this topic, get the books or tapes of leaders who do this well and go to school on them. You owe it to your people to learn to address this subject with clarity and wisdom.

RESOURCES AND THE INFORMATION PRINCIPLE

DURING THE EARLY THEATER days of Willow I had no shortage of ineptitude when it came to dealing with the subject of money. One of my biggest mistakes was that I failed to give people adequate information.

Once, when we were so far behind our weekly budget that I saw virtually no hope for financial survival, either for the church or for Lynne and me personally, I decided to do something drastic. At the close of a Sunday morning sermon, I announced to the whole congregation that I was going away for a while. "I can no longer handle the financial pressures of this church," I said. "I have to get away to think this over, and I'm not sure when I'm coming back. Something has to change because we're going under financially and it doesn't seem like anyone cares but me."

With that brilliant display of leadership, I walked off the platform. Within seconds I was surrounded by at least thirty people who were all saying the same thing: "We didn't know. Why didn't you tell us? Why didn't you let us help? We love this church. We want to be part of the solution."

Huddled at the bottom of the stage stairs, these genuinely concerned people asked some very intelligent questions about the church's financial condition. "What does the weekly offering need to be? Exactly where does the money go? Who makes the decisions? Who is planning the future budget? How can we turn this around?"

That day I got a crash course on the Information Principle. People want to know. They deserve to know. They can't help unless they know.

From that day forward I have chosen to lay everything out in front of our people, and I do mean everything. At Willow we have concluded that there is no good reason to be secretive about finances, so we have an absolutely open-book policy.

Each year on Vision Night I announce to the congregation the budget established by our board of directors. I use as many visuals as possible to make it clear where we are as a church and where we are headed in the future. Then I allow time for questions and answers, and no question is off limits. In addition, anybody can get a fully audited statement that explains where every dime given to Willow Creek Community Church has gone.

As you can tell, I'm a fanatic about full financial disclosure. Why? Because anything less than full disclosure tends to create suspicion, and nothing shuts off the resource faucet quicker than suspicion. If there is nothing to hide, why be secretive? Why not just lay it all out there? At Willow, there's not a single thing that we're ashamed of, nothing that we need to keep hidden. I strongly advise every church leader to operate this way.

RESOURCES AND THE KISS PRINCIPLE

MOST PEOPLE HAVE HEARD about this one. The Kiss Principle means: "Keep it Simple, Stupid."

Experience has taught me that the archenemy of fundraising is complexity. When I hear of churches trying to organize multiple, simultaneous fund drives—complete with car washes, walk-a-thons, and pancake breakfasts sponsored by competing sub-ministries—I feel like shouting a warning: "Don't do it!" From what I have seen, complexity in fundraising is one of the most effective ways to shut people down. Not only is it confusing, but it also fosters the perception that the church always has its hand out.

Parenthetically, I believe that half of the fundraising strategies employed in these churches are unbiblical. I'm sorry, that's the way I see it. The Bible doesn't teach that a church ought to be financed by bake sales or bingo. (And I'm not really sorry.)

People at Willow need to understand just two sets of numbers. The first set is our budgeted weekly offering versus our actual weekly offering. Each week we print the current budgeted and actual numbers in the weekly newsletter we distribute at our midweek services. That way every member can monitor exactly how we are doing.

The second set of numbers that Willow people need to follow is associated with our year-end challenge. Each year as we approach

Thanksgiving and Christmas, we present to the congregation the special needs of our inner city partnerships and the international arm of the Willow Creek Association. We might also ask the congregation to give sacrificially toward additional property purchases or building programs. During this annual six-week challenge we present a specific financial goal, and each week we keep the congregation informed of our progress toward that goal. But we don't drag the process out for months, and we break our backs to keep it simple.[2]

Let me add that I also apply the KISS Principle to financial reporting practices. If I get a board report or a spreadsheet from our finance department that I can't understand, I send it back. I remind them that I am a pastor, not a CPA, and I ask them to "idiot proof" it for me. If I can't grasp it, how will I ever be able to inform our congregation about it? How will I make it through congregational Q&A times that often include financial inquiries?

When it comes to finances, complexity kills.

RESOURCES AND THE PRINCIPLE OF STRATEGIC DISCIPLING

IN ALMOST EVERY CHURCH there are people afflicted with affluence. Unfortunately, most leaders don't know how to relate to such people.

Many pastors are so intimidated by wealthy folks that they steer clear of them to shield their own insecurity. Others are so concerned about staying completely impartial with regard to the haves and the have-nots that they avoid wealthy people like the plague. Still others, with personal agendas in mind, buddy up to wealthy folks in hopes of receiving perks for themselves and maybe a little money for the church.

---

[2]In November of 2000 we did our first ever three-year Capital Campaign. The details of this are available on Defining Moments Tape: Capital Campaign # DF 0102.

But sooner or later, every leader has to decide how he or she is going to relate to people with heavy doses of resources. My approach, over the years, has been to meet with people with significant resources to challenge them to get into the game. If they're far from God, I try to lead them into a saving relationship with Jesus Christ as I would anybody. If they are spiritually immature, I try to help them grow up. If they are loners, I encourage them to join a small group so they can experience Christian community. If they are on the sidelines, I try to help them discover their spiritual gifts so they can become fully engaged in the work of the church. In short, I try to disciple them. Along the way, I also remind them of the words of Jesus, who said, "To whom much is given, much is required."

Over the years my bottom-line message to wealthy Christians has been that with a big net worth comes a huge kingdom responsibility. If they're open, I explain further what that means. Some (but not all) wealthy people have the spiritual gift of giving, but few understand the implications of that. I inform them that Scripture teaches that people with the spiritual gift of giving are challenged to earn as much money as they can, live frugally, and flow as much money as possible into God's work in this world. That's the essence of the spiritual gift of giving (Romans 12:8).

Leaders need to stand toe-to-toe with resourced people who have the gift of giving and say, "God gave you this gift for a reason. You're as accountable for the development and full utilization of that gift as I am for the gift God gave me."

Many years ago I spoke with a man at Willow who, by his own admission, had the spiritual gift of giving. Earlier he had bragged to me that he only had to work one or two days a week and that he golfed the rest of the time. Prompted by the Holy Spirit, I asked him if he was developing his gift of giving to the peak of its potential. I told him that I live with an almost overwhelming feeling of responsibility for the three gifts that God has given me: Leadership, Evangelism, and Teaching. I explained how badly I want to hear the commendation from God, "Well done, Bill. You optimized the spiritual gifts I entrusted to you. Good job!"

Then I turned the challenge his way, asking him if he was ready to take his spiritual gift of giving as seriously as I was taking my gifts.

To his credit, he accepted that challenge and began to give far beyond his weekly tithe. For the last ten years, he has tracked me down every Christmas Eve and given me an envelope with a sizable check designated for our outreach ministries. "As long as you keep faithful with your gifts," he tells me, "I'll keep faithful with mine. We're in this together, brother." I always write him back and thank him for taking his gift seriously.

One of the jobs of leaders is to help people with the spiritual gift of giving get into the game and understand that they are responsible to God for the "much they have been given."

Every time I can help a rich young ruler break free from the tyranny of greed so that he or she can leverage resources for that which matters most, I feel like I've been used by God to do something very important. People who have been discipled and challenged to use their gifts of giving can do serious kingdom good for the rest of their lives.

Recently, we received one of the largest gifts ever received in the history of our church. It was given by an individual who believes wholeheartedly in the mission of the local church. When he saw what the Willow Creek Association was doing to train church leaders worldwide he was moved to give. I have his permission to share what he wrote on the note accompanying his gift.

> Over the last eight months, God has opened my eyes to the "what" and the "why" of Willow. At the same time, God has been educating me in what has been very obvious to you for a long time, that the local church really is the hope of the world.

So I want to be one of those who help finance this phase of the development of the WCA. This is the kind of giving opportunity I've been dying to find. Receive this gift with great love and use it in whatever way would profit the kingdom most.

There are a lot of people like the person who wrote this note, people with the gift of giving who have "been dying to find" an opportunity to give to something they really believe in. All that is holding many of them back is that they have never been discipled, never been invited into the game, never been challenged to take their gift seriously. Leaders, it's our job to do that.

RESOURCES AND THE VISION PRINCIPLE

I DON'T KNOW IF you've ever noticed it, but very few people get fired up about financing mundane needs. I don't blame them. If they're like me, they want to invest their limited funds in a vision far grander than paying utility bills, restocking janitorial supplies, or maintaining the church copy machine. They're not going to put their annual bonus in the Christmas Eve offering unless they have some assurance that it's going to make a significant difference in the world. They want to know that their hard-earned money will be used to fund authentic ministry that impacts real people.

During Willow's recent capital campaign, my wife and I wrote out the largest check of our lives. We gave the check with great joy and enthusiasm. Why? Because we were genuinely excited about the good our gift would do. We knew that part of it would fund expanded facilities on our campus; a portion of it would underwrite the cost of a Regional Ministry Strategy that will touch thousands of people in the greater Chicago area; some would make it possible for Willow's Extension Ministries to serve more people living in conditions of poverty; and the remainder would allow the Willow Creek Association to train more church leaders all around the world.

We knew this because the leadership at Willow had cast a clear vision of Willow's future. They told stories, showed pictures, wrote songs, and led us in prayers that made our hearts burn for these causes. When the time came to write out our check, our only frustration was that we couldn't do more.

That's the Vision Principle in action.

People don't give to organizations or to other people. They give to visions. When leaders who understand this take the time to paint pictures for people and to help them imagine the kingdom good that will result from their collective efforts, then people are free to release their resources joyfully. And generally, the grander the vision, the greater the giving.

Recently I was challenging a new man in our community to help the Willow Creek Association. Because he was unfamiliar with the ministry of the Association, he wisely took the time to ask exactly what we would do with his money. Over the lunch table I gave him our vision.

"We want to help every church on planet Earth reach its full redemptive potential," I told him. "We want to see churches led by leaders, taught by teachers, and administrated by administrators. We want to help church leaders establish clear missions and values so they can reach lost people in their communities and guide them toward spiritual maturity. Until our dying breath we want to help the bride of Christ become a force against which the very gates of hell cannot prevail."

When I finally stopped talking, he was wide-eyed. "That's huge!" he said.

"You bet your life it is," I answered. "And we need some huge investors to turn this vision into reality. Will you pray and find out if God wants you to help us?"

He prayed and God prompted him to put some of his resources behind our vision. But what would have happened if I had told him that our vision was to provide new choir robes to comatose churches or to re-pad the pews of churches that exist only for the already convinced? My guess is that such a vision would have failed to capture his heart. People love to give to compelling visions, to grand, God-honoring visions that promise to make a significant difference in this world.

So when you are raising resources for the local church, remind people that you are building something that represents the hope of the world. Cast exciting, stretching, God-honoring visions. Paint brilliant pictures in peoples' minds. Then pray like crazy and be prepared—because people will give more than you think.

Before closing this chapter, I'd like to offer some guidelines for resourcing a church staff.

STAFF RESOURCES: THE FAIR EXCHANGE GUIDELINE

IN LUKE 10:7 JESUS teaches that a laborer is worthy of his or her hire. What this says to church leaders is that staff members should be paid fairly. Those who serve the church faithfully in significant ways should be paid accordingly.

In my opinion, the caliber of people needed to provide competent senior leadership for the church of the future will force most congregations to totally rethink their compensation programs. The Fair Exchange Guideline recently prompted us to do this at Willow.

After evaluating our staff, we concluded that we had many competent, godly people working tirelessly for the kingdom whose pay was not in proportion to the magnitude of their contribution. So we commissioned a Compensation Committee to overhaul the entire pay structure until the Holy Spirit gave us peace regarding the fairness of compensation. Though it took nearly a year to complete this process, our elders and board of directors rightly believed that we owed our staff this careful evaluation and the resulting salary increases.

STAFF RESOURCES: THE UNMUZZLED OX GUIDELINE

IN DEUTERONOMY 25:4, God says, "Do not muzzle an ox while it is treading out the grain." For our purposes that could be translated like this: Give staff members the tools they need to do what you're asking them to do.

As the CRR, a leader is responsible for making sure that his or her staff members have what they need to do their jobs well. The only way to do that is to ask the right questions. "What do you need in order to multiply your impact? Do you need more space in the building? Additional ministry dollars? Better equipment? Further training? Computers? Part-time help?"

Staff members need to know that the CRR is doing everything in his or her power to come up with the tools they need to flourish.

Once during the early days of Willow our music director became very discouraged. He had been providing music for all our services on a tired out, secondhand Wurlitzer electric piano with a half dozen keys out of commission. The frustration was killing him. One day I heard him pounding on that keyboard, trying to get a particular key to work and shouting, "This is crazy! I can't take this anymore! How can anybody expect me to do decent music with this piece of junk?"

I was still convinced that his specialty pencils were unnecessary, but even I knew that the piano situation was getting critical. I walked from my office into his tiny workspace and said, "Look Dave, if you'll keep writing music and building the vocal team, I'll try to solve the piano problem. Just give me a little time."

Of course we had no money for a piano. We were still making $5.00 payments for the office carpet. So I prayed, "God, I have a teammate with a need only you can meet. Please, somehow, come through for us."

A few weeks later a new family from the church invited Lynne and me over for dinner. I walked into their living room and there it was—a shiny, black, baby grand piano! All during dinner I kept eyeing that piano. Every once in a while, even though the conversation wasn't about music, I'd ask a question about the piano. "How long have you had your piano?" And then, ever so subtly, "Does anyone play it, or is it mainly for decoration?" Lynne caught on and began kicking me under the table.

Finally, at the end of the night, our host said what all older people say to young struggling pastors, "If there's ever anything we can do for you . . ." Before he had time to finish his sentence I blurted out, "We need a piano! One just about like that one!" Lynne almost fainted. She had that shocked look on her face that said, "I can't believe this. I can't take him anywhere!"

But about a week later our dinner host called and said that he and his wife had discussed it, and they would love to donate their piano to the church. They preferred to think of their beautiful piano leading people into worship rather than collecting dust in their living room.

I'll never forget the day they hired a piano mover and delivered that black baby grand to our church offices. The look on Dave's face when that piano rolled across the threshold said it all. Not only was he in awe of God's grace in meeting his music need so spectacularly, but he was deeply grateful to me for taking his need seriously and for going out of my way to find the tool that would help him multiply the impact of his ministry.

A leader's efforts to secure necessary tools for staff members inevitably builds morale and rapport on teams. It also deepens the leader's faith in God's ability to provide for staff needs. Time and time again I have seen God open the windows of heaven to supply every conceivable kind of tool for enhancing the impact of our staff team.

STAFF RESOURCES: THE DOUBLE HONOR GUIDELINE

IN 1 TIMOTHY 5:17, PAUL instructs the church to give double honor to those who lead and teach well. In today's parlance that means,

"Bless the socks off your key players. Find out what would thrill their hearts, and then turn over heaven and earth to bless them with it."

Willow has an unbelievable staff. Through the years, in response to the Double Honor Guideline, my Executive Pastor and I have arranged for scores of double honor gifts: extra vacation time, appropriate financial bonuses, interesting travel opportunities, and unusual training options. I'm on the constant lookout for whatever will communicate double honor to staff members who have completed a particularly challenging ministry season or met a uniquely demanding goal.

I don't want to just resource staff members' ministries. I want to resource their souls. That's why I practice the principle of double honor.

PAYING PASTORS: THE WISDOM GUIDELINE

PEOPLE OFTEN FEEL CONFLICTED about the issue of paying the pastor. Some folks immediately think about the apostle Paul making tents so he wouldn't be a financial drain to the early Christians. Too many of these people, who often serve on church boards, are what I call pup-tent people. They want their pastor to make pup tents, sleep in pup tents, die in pup tents—you get the point.

In stark contrast to the pup-tent crowd are those who believe the words of TV's prosperity preachers. Elders and deacons of this ilk are convinced that a pastor with a huge bank account, and often an ego to match, brings honor both to God and to the church. The result is scandalous pastoral salaries and perks.

Most church boards fall somewhere between these extremes, and most pastors are themselves as conflicted as anybody else. On one hand they believe they ought to do some suffering for the cause of Christ. The thought of spiritual leaders before them who actually shed blood to further the kingdom make their sacrifices seem paltry in comparison. On the other hand the kids need braces, the roof leaks, the brakes on the car are shot. How can pastors make ends meet without reasonable pay?

The one principle I want to suggest in regard to paying the pastor is called the Wisdom Guideline and it comes right from the lips of Jesus. "Be as wise as serpents," he said, "and as innocent as doves" (Matthew 10:16).

This guideline challenges everybody engaged in the salary discussion to exercise sober-mindedness and old-fashioned wisdom. It means carefully assessing all the variables related to the pastor's salary: What is the size of the congregation? How large is the staff? What is the scope of responsibility? How many years of faithful service have been rendered? Has the pastor shown consistent improvement in leading and preaching? Are there special family needs? The list could go on.

This guideline assumes that Spirit-filled people will talk openly, lovingly, and constructively about these issues until everyone around the table (including the pastor) reaches consensus, until everyone can honestly say, "Together we have sought God's wisdom and we believe he has led us." The goal is to come up with an ample but not scandalous provision for the pastor that can pass the "sniff test" of people both inside and outside the church.

I want to end this chapter on a very personal note. For the twenty-seven years I have been the pastor of Willow Creek Community Church, I have been treated very kindly by our elders and board members. In the early years of the church they could not pay me and that broke their hearts. As the church got stronger financially they joyfully began to compensate me in accordance with the Wisdom Guideline.

In addition to an appropriate salary, Willow has also provided me and my family with health and medical coverage and a generous retirement program. I have also been given adequate workspace, the books and resources I need for sermon preparation, and training opportunities to help me grow as a teacher and leader. In fact, to my recollection, anytime I have requested anything that would enhance my ministry, the answer has always been, "Yes."

Additionally, I have been given a small expense account so I can take staff and lay leaders out for appreciation dinners. (They watch that expense account like hawks, and it hasn't been raised in fifteen years, but it's there!) I've also been afforded reliable transportation through an arrangement with a local car dealership. And I have been given the world's best executive assistant to help me do what I do.

Finally, the provision that I probably appreciate more than any other is my annual summer study break. Years ago I started with one week; now I'm usually out of the church office for almost eight weeks each summer. During these weeks I continue to lead the ministry through phone calls, faxes, emails, and off-site meetings with staff teams, but my work schedule is greatly reduced and leaves plenty of time for reading, recreation, and relationships. Not only does this time away recharge my emotional, physical, and spiritual batteries, but in hindsight I realize it was one of the single greatest contributors to my family life. I am convinced that part of the reason my grown children love God and the church, and love Lynne and me and each other, is that every summer during their childhood Willow offered us time to relax together as a family.

What I'm saying is that I feel like the most blessed pastor on the planet. The level of care I've received throughout the years motivates me to give increasing amounts of time and energy back to the church. Isn't that how it should be? I long for the day when every pastor of every church is treated the same way I am, and is free to feel the same gratitude and motivation I feel.

How can I sum up this chapter? I guess the bottom line is this: Leaders, don't shy away from the resource challenge. Plunge into it. Learn from it. Let God stretch your faith because of it. And then, dream with me of the day when a river of resources will be pouring into local churches all around the world so that the work of God can flourish.

CHAPTER SIX

Developing Emerging Leaders

When Leaders Are at Their Best

THESE DAYS THERE ARE FEW MINISTRY OPPORTUNITIES I ENJOY MORE than holing up in an interesting location with a dozen other church leaders to wrestle with the challenges of leadership. One question I am apt to pose during our discussions is, "When are leaders at their best?" This question always generates animated conversation, in part because there are so many acceptable answers.

One person usually begins by suggesting that leaders are at their best when they are performing the functions of leadership— casting God-honoring visions, building teams, setting goals, solving problems, and raising resources. When they are modeling exemplary leadership, *that's* when leaders shine.

Someone else quickly reminds the group that leadership involves more than just demonstrating skills. Leaders must exhibit character. When leaders manifest traits like trustworthiness, fair-mindedness, humility, servanthood, and endurance over a long period of time, and when they prove themselves to be unwavering in crisis, *that's* when leaders are at their best.

About that time, another voice pipes in adding that what matters more than anything is the spiritual component of leadership.

Leaders are at their best when they are working in tandem with God. When they are humbly bowed before the Heavenly Father, acknowledging his sovereignty, listening to his promptings, submitting to his leadership, and then courageously carrying out his orders, *that's* when leaders are at their best.

When the energy level in the room gets high enough, I weigh in with my opinion, "I think leaders are at their very best when they are raising up leaders around them. Or put another way, leaders are at their best when they are creating a leadership culture."

When I see a leader whose radar wand is spinning around to locate an emerging leader, or when I watch an older leader investing time and energy to coach and empower a younger leader, I am convinced that I am seeing leadership at its very best.

I am also convinced that leaders must make this one of their highest priorities. Why? Because only leaders can develop other leaders and create a leadership culture. Teachers can't do it. Administrators can't do it. Mercy-gifted folks can't do it. Only leaders can multiply the leadership impact by raising up additional leaders.

Think about it. When a leader develops not only his or her own leadership potential, but draws out the leadership potential of scores of other leaders as well, the kingdom impact from one life is multiplied exponentially. It produces far more fruit than any single leadership achievement could have. The impact of that leader's life will be felt for many generations to come. Can you see why I believe this is what defines leadership at its best?

In this chapter I'd like to explain how a leader creates a leadership culture and leaves a legacy of well-trained leaders.

LEADERSHIP DEVELOPMENT REQUIRES A VISION

NOTHING THIS IMPORTANT CAN be achieved without a vision. Trust me. Leadership development *never* happens accidentally. It only happens when some leader has a white-hot vision for it, when his or her pulse rate doubles at the very thought of pumping into the organizational system a steady stream of competent leaders.

Before we developed a clear vision for leadership development at Willow, we fell into the trap that catches many churches, the trap of urgent demands. For years, almost all our efforts went into meeting the immediate challenge of the next service, the next outreach event, the next extension effort for the poor, the next building program. We rarely paused long enough to wonder about future leaders. *How will we identify them? Who will develop them? Will they be prepared to face the challenges of tomorrow?*

Believe me, in high-speed, high-intensity organizations—and most churches I know in the Willow Creek Association and in other church cultures fit that description perfectly—leadership development will always slip to the bottom of the agenda unless mature leaders force it to the top.

This is a current growth edge for us at Willow. While we have finally developed a clear vision for leadership development, we're still in the early stage of owning that vision. Some of our senior leaders embrace it wholeheartedly; others aren't quite there yet. Recently an outside group of consultants used the phrase "a necessary nuisance" to describe how many of our staff view leadership development. Though it was disheartening to hear that these people consider leadership development a *nuisance,* the fact that they consider it *necessary* is a step in the right direction.

A few years ago I was reminiscing with our director of small groups about Willow's twentieth anniversary celebration, which was held at the United Center in downtown Chicago. He said, "Wouldn't it be something if someday we had so many small group leaders that we had to use the United Center for our annual small group leaders' retreat? Can you imagine having 20,000 small group leaders?" For me, envisioning that was like receiving an injection of adrenalin.

Imagine how strong a church would be if it had a deep bench of competent leaders in every area of its ministry, from small groups to children's ministry to spiritual formation. That will only happen if leaders shape a compelling vision. At Willow we are a long way from needing the United Center for our small group leaders' retreat, but every year we have to search for a larger facility to accommodate our ever-increasing leadership core. And who knows, after another ten or fifteen years of leadership development, we might spend a day or two where Michael Jordan made basketball history.

Creating a vision, of course, is just the beginning. The next challenge is to come up with a strategy for turning that vision into reality. To prompt our thinking about such a plan, let me pose a question: How is it that you wound up becoming a leader?

There are many possible answers to this question, but in talking with many leaders I have discovered three common themes. These themes provide the basis for a practical strategy for developing leaders.

SOMEONE SPOTTED OUR POTENTIAL

WHETHER YOU REMEMBER IT or not, it's highly likely that at some point in your past somebody noticed something in your wiring pattern that you probably didn't even know was there. Putting a hand on your shoulder, that person said, "I think you could be a leader."

For me, this person was my dad. From the time I was just a little guy, he told me I was a leader. To build on that potential he intentionally threw me into all kinds of challenging, high-risk situations, even at a very early age. His parting words were always, "You're a leader. You'll figure it out." Actually, I suspect that was an excuse for him to avoid having to coach or train me in anything. His leadership development course consisted of hurling me into the deep end of the pool and shouting, "Sink or swim!"

Years later a Christian camp director saw leadership potential in me. He put me on an accelerated training track by making me a leader of other leaders when I was still a teenager. I remember questioning his judgment on that. I asked him why he thought other leaders twice my age would ever follow my direction. He said, "Bill, leadership is more a function of ability than age. You provide competent leadership and people of any age will follow your direction." That advice served me well that summer and came to mind often during the early years of Willow.

Think back. Wasn't that how it started for you? Didn't somebody detect leadership potential in you and then tell you to step up to the challenge?

SOMEONE INVESTED IN US

A SECOND COMMON THEME that leaders identify in the journey toward leadership is that someone invested in us. Perhaps the person who first saw leadership potential in us also developed us. Or maybe someone else along the way actually did the developmental work. But all of us got to where we are today because someone built into us, coached us, and showed us how to lead.

Years ago Dr. Gilbert Bilezikian, the college professor whose compelling vision of the church first drew me into the ministry, also became a significant leadership mentor for me. He taught me about servant leadership, about the uses (and dangers) of power, about managing conflict, and about building consensus on teams. I often wonder where I would be as a leader had I not been taught those invaluable lessons early in my ministry.

All the effective leaders I have ever talked to can point back to someone who sacrificed time and energy to grow them up as leaders. The gift those people gave us is something we should never take for granted.

Recently, after a long day of church work, I was walking through the parking lot to my car. In the distance I saw Dr. Bilezikian. I got into my car and pulled up alongside him. "Gil, I was just a kid when you agreed to meet with me after class at Trinity College. I was just a kid when you invited me to your home in Wheaton and fixed meals for me and talked for hours and hours about the church. I was just a kid when you let me call you late at night when I was having a leadership struggle. But the investment you made in me changed my life."

He smiled widely and with a twinkle in his eye said, "Ahh . . . you're still just a kid! But thanks!"

We need to remember and to honor the people who made these priceless investments in our leadership development. Then we need to let those memories motivate us to play the same role in another leader's life.

SOMEONE TRUSTED US WITH RESPONSIBILITY

LEADERS MENTION A THIRD common theme when asked how they became leaders. Someone took a risk and said, "Here's the leadership baton. I think you're ready to run with it. Here's a job. I believe you can do it. Here's a position. I'm confident you can fill it." Hopefully, they offered a little coaching when we were first starting out and stuck around long enough to ensure that we would succeed. But leaders don't become leaders until someone actually puts a baton of responsibility in their hand and says, "Go!"

So a leadership development plan has to address these three phases:

1. Identifying emerging leaders
2. Investing in the development of emerging leaders
3. Entrusting responsibility to emerging leaders

JESUS' LEADERSHIP DEVELOPMENT PLAN

FROM WHAT I READ in Scripture, Jesus moved through these three phases as he raised up his disciples and other potential leaders. First, consider how he selected his disciples. He didn't just say, "Here's a line. First twelve guys that step across it get picked." No, he selected his disciples carefully. He took his time and prayed fervently before he chose them. He knew that in the not-too-distant future, he would be handing the leadership of the New Testament church over to them. He had to make sure that he chose people with the potential to assume that responsibility.

After Jesus identified all twelve, he very quickly moved into an intense time of investing into their lives. He spent time with them. He taught them. He nurtured them. He confronted them. He motivated them. He rebuked them. He inspired them.

Then months later, when he knew the time was right, he moved into the third phase of leadership development. He entrusted them with real ministry responsibility and coached them into effectiveness.

His plan worked marvelously and it's worth emulating.

I sometimes wonder how much impact the church would be having in this world if church leaders were more intentional about leadership development. More leaders could launch more ministries that could meet more needs. More lives could be transformed spiritually. More marriages and families could be restored. More resources could be distributed to the poor. Can you even imagine? In twenty years, the world could be a different place.

But that won't happen unless we commit ourselves to finding potential leaders and developing them.

In the next few pages I want to describe the character qualities I look for in emerging leaders.

THE FIRST NECESSARY QUALITY IS INFLUENCE

POTENTIAL LEADERS ALWAYS HAVE a natural ability to influence others. Even if they have no conscious intention of leading people, they automatically exert influence.

I don't have to be in a group of people for long before I can identify the men and the women who influence the rest of the group. It becomes apparent whose ideas capture the attention of the others, whose suggestions become the marching orders, whose wisdom is most respected.

Leadership, at its core, is about influence. So I'm always looking for people who have the ability to influence their peers.

THE SECOND QUALITY IS CHARACTER

LOTS OF PEOPLE WITH influence lack the character to use that influence constructively or Christianly. Once I spot someone with influence, I try to discern whether he or she has the honesty, the humility, the stability, the teachability, and the integrity to steward that influence well. Because I'm usually looking for church leaders, I want to see evidence of a sincere walk with God, a yieldedness to the Holy Spirit, and a commitment to the authority of God's Word.

When I meet a person who appears to have both influence and solid character I intensify my search for the remaining three qualities.

THE THIRD QUALITY IS PEOPLE SKILLS

MY DEFINITION OF "people skills" includes sensitivity to the thoughts and the feelings of others, and the ability to listen—and I mean *really* listen—to the ideas of others. I'm looking for people who genuinely care for other people, who view others as more than a means to an end.

Some years ago I had lunch with the man who many predict will be the next CEO of Disney. What struck me more than any of his other impressive leadership skills was his relational aptitude. He listened well and complimented other team members warmly. He gave every evidence of being able to pass any relational intelligence test with flying colors.

Top leaders must have people skills. They must be able to relate winsomely to a wide range of people, to folks with personality quirks, power issues, and self-esteem deficiencies. So I always look for leaders with well-developed people skills.

THE FOURTH QUALITY IS DRIVE

I ALSO LOOK FOR action-oriented people who are comfortable taking initiative. These are the kind of people who at restaurants are the first ones to say, "Let's order. Let's get the show on the road."

Once I was invited by the CEO of a very large corporation to join him and his senior executive team for dinner. He had selected a very expensive restaurant and reserved a private room. This extremely sophisticated establishment had all the symbols of fine dining, including a tuxedo-clad waiter with a fake European accent and a towel draped over his arm. Apparently this guy saw us as his captive audience, and he started a lengthy speech about the history of the restaurant, its recent renovations, and what a wonderful dining experience we were about to enjoy.

I thought my CEO host was going to jump out of his skin. This dinner was just one of five agenda items he had to cross off yet that night. Finally he couldn't stand it any longer. He broke into the promotional talk and said, "Excuse me. I'm sorry to interrupt you, but we're in a bit of a rush. Would you please go into the kitchen and bring out whatever is hot so we can eat right away? I know that all the food is wonderful here, so I don't care what you bring as long as you can bring it fast. Thank you very much."

That CEO was not trying to be rude. But he was not about to let the length of that dining experience imperil the other agenda items needing attention that night. So he took immediate action. He initiated a change in the plans. I'm not suggesting that there's anything wrong with lengthy dining experiences; when the time is right they can be wonderful. My point is that good leaders make things happen.

In traffic, action-oriented people spend most of their time in the passing lane. In a supermarket they're the ones pulling groceries from the shelves without ever breaking stride because they want to finish the job so they can move on to something more important than shopping.

I often tell potential staff members at Willow that I'm not looking for fifty-watt bulbs. I'm not looking for seventy-five watt bulbs. I'm looking for hundred-watt bulbs that will burn all night long if need be. What I'm talking about is drive. I'm talking about people who have so much energy that they energize others without even trying.

My life verse is 1 Corinthians 15:58. "Be steadfast, immovable, always abounding in the work of the Lord." I'm looking for leaders with the drive necessary to abound in the work of the Lord. When I find such people, I'm highly motivated to invest my time and energy in their development.

THE FINAL QUALITY IS INTELLIGENCE

WHEN I SAY I look for intelligence, I don't necessarily mean that I look for high SAT scores or a sheepskin from an Ivy League university. What I look for in potential leaders is mental quickness. I look for people with street smarts, with the kind of mental savvy required to process lots of information, sift through it, consider all the options, and generally make the right decision. I also look for someone with an eager, curious mind—intellectual elasticity, I call it—who can learn and grow over the long haul.

These five leadership indicators—influence, character, relational skills, drive, and intelligence—do not form an exhaustive list. But they provide a good framework for an initial evaluation. When I find people with all or most of these qualities, I start figuring out ways to get these folks in my orbit so I can get to know them better and verify my initial observations. If I discover they have "the stuff" I'm looking for I do my best to get them on a developmental track as soon as possible.

Now let's look at beginning a leadership development plan of your own.

PHASE 1: DRAW UP YOUR OWN TOP-FIVE QUALITY LIST

LET ME SUGGEST AN assignment that I believe will help you customize a leadership development plan for your own setting. First, to define the qualities that are important to you in identifying emerging leaders, why not take the list I suggested and hold a special meeting with your leadership team? Together, decide if the identification criteria I use are appropriate for your setting. Personalize the list with whatever additions or deletions your team decides on. The goal of the exercise is for you and your team to establish the criterion that will help you identify emerging leaders around you.

Next, I suggest that you do what we did recently at a management team meeting. Using a flip chart, we wrote the words "EMERGING LEADERS AT WILLOW" across the top of a huge sheet of paper. Then we asked team members to fill the empty page with names of people with great leadership potential. Within half an hour, we had several pages filled with names of emerging leaders. For the next hour we discussed ways to get those people on developmental tracks that could help them actualize their full leadership potential.

PHASE 2: INVEST IN EMERGING LEADERS

ONCE YOUR TOP-FIVE quality list is in place and you've identified people with leadership potential, the next step is investment. This is the intentional development or training stage.

Exactly *how* to do this most effectively is a hotly debated issue in leadership development theories these days. I've read dozens of books on this topic and even experts disagree. Some argue for a curriculum-driven leadership development process: "Get them in a classroom. Teach them leadership."

Other experts say, "Nonsense. Forget the classroom. What is needed is a mentoring process. Leaders need on-the-job training."

Still other experts advise, "Just identify high-potential leaders, give them a job to do, and they'll discover what it means to be a leader all by themselves." (That was my dad's approach; just throw the kid out there and let him figure it out!)

While theories of leadership development differ, this much is certain: It takes a leader to develop a leader. You can take that one to the bank. Let me say it again: *Leaders learn best from other leaders.*

I usually hesitate when people ask me to participate in leadership development programs. "How's it going to work?" I ask. If they respond in the typical fashion—"We're going to get Joe Shmo [with a Ph.D. in this or that] to teach on leadership"—I tell them the same thing I tell everybody else. "Most good leaders aren't going to want to participate in that program because Joe Shmo isn't a leader. He's a classroom teacher. He might be a great teacher, but he has never really led anything. True leaders want more than theory from teacher types. They want to be around other leaders who have actually been in the game, leaders with a few bloodstains on their uniforms."

For emerging leaders to become seasoned, wise, and effective leaders, they need proximity to and interaction with veteran leaders. This can happen in a dozen different ways, but it must happen. In Jesus' day it was common for leaders-in-training to simply follow the veteran leader around. They would talk together, walk together, eat their meals together, sleep in neighboring tents. They would spend months, sometimes years, apprenticing. This allowed them to internalize the vision and values of the veteran leader in ways that served them the rest of their lives.

Though that approach to leadership development was basic and time-intensive, it was very effective. I'm not sure a better approach has been discovered in the centuries since then. Present lifestyles and working patterns make that approach seem, on the surface, impractical. But the truth is, there is no substitute for personal investment. Those of us who are more seasoned in leadership must order our lives in such a way that we can carve out time to invest in the next generation of leaders. It is our responsibility. We imperil the church and our world if we don't take that responsibility seriously.

I was shocked to learn that Jack Welch, the former CEO of General Electric, spent (fasten your seat belts!) thirty percent of his time doing leadership development with emerging leaders at General Electric. Thirty percent!

In my interviewing and speaking with top corporate leaders around the country, I've been surprised to learn how much of their time is devoted to leadership development.

Jim Mellado, the president of the Willow Creek Association, has been a constant nag (or as Proverbs says, "a dripping faucet") regarding this matter. He has been relentless in urging me to invest more of my time in mentoring pastors and leaders who have high potential. So in recent years I've doubled the amount of time I spend on this. Currently I devote about ten days a year to mentoring groups of emerging church leaders.

On each of these mentoring days I meet with a group of ten to twelve leaders. The format is loose. At the outset I share a few leadership lessons I've learned along the way. Then I open the conversation up for discussion, and we spend the rest of the day trying to help each other overcome the leadership challenges we are all facing.

It never fails. After leading one of these day-long mentoring sessions I always drive home convinced that I made the most valuable contribution to the kingdom that I could possibly have made that day. When the evaluations come back, they're often so moving that Jim reads them to me, to his staff, and to the board of directors of the WCA to remind everyone of the importance of leadership development. These mentoring sessions are some of the highest rated events we do.

How veteran leaders choose to invest in emerging leaders will vary greatly. Some leaders might start (as I am) by mentoring small groups of young leaders. Others might develop curriculum to be used in mentoring situations. Some might teach and write more on the subject of leadership.

But whatever we choose to do, this basic truth stands: Leaders learn best from other leaders. It is the responsibility of veteran leaders to provide the necessary opportunities so the next generation of leaders will be trained and ready to meet the challenges of the future.

PHASE 3: ENTRUST EMERGING LEADERS WITH RESPONSIBILITY

ASK LEADERSHIP DEVELOPMENT EXPERTS what is the best catalyst for a leader's growth and they will all answer in unison: "Make him or her lead something." No one can grow as a leader without the real life challenges of actually leading.

After Jesus had identified and invested in his emerging leaders, the moment came when he said, "Pack your bags, fellows. It's show time. It's make-it or break-it time. It's sink-or-swim time."

And Jesus didn't seek to minimize the challenge he gave his followers. Remember his words in Matthew 10:16? "I am sending you out like sheep among wolves." What was Jesus saying? "This is the real deal. The stakes are high. The possibility of failure is real. And I'm not going to protect you from all risk. You've got to step out. You've got to lead." And they did!

Here's the point: When we have identified emerging leaders, and when we have built into them, trained them, and adequately prepared them, then we must entrust these folks with real responsibilities. We must hand emerging leaders an *important* kingdom baton—not a little make-believe job or a low-stakes challenge—but something that will make their pulse quicken; something that will make them feel believed in, valued, and held in high esteem; something that will make them fall to their knees and cry out for God's help; something that will demand the best they have to offer.

The truth is that we leaders live for high-stake challenges! We crave the kind of kingdom goals that make us gasp and gulp. That's not true of non-leaders; they generally prefer to keep challenge (and stress) levels low; that's how God made them. But leaders want the kind of kingdom responsibilities that demand everything they've got.

Anything less than that is de-motivating. So we owe our emerging leaders exciting high-stake kingdom leadership opportunities.

Everywhere I travel throughout the world, I meet competent church staff and fired-up lay people. These folks ooze leadership potential; it's obvious a mile away. But many of these people have all but given up on ever being trusted with a great kingdom challenge. I look at them while I'm speaking on leadership and I see that familiar longing in their eyes. I know what they're thinking: "If someone would just make an investment in me, if someone would just train me, if someone would just give me a chance—I know I could make a difference with my life. I know I could lead something worth leading. And I would do everything in my power to lead it effectively. If someone would just give me the opportunity."

Recently a businessman friend of mine called and said, "I was thanking God for you this morning. The thing I most appreciate about you, Bill, is that you invited me in the game. For years I sat on the bench at Willow. But you told me to suit up and start preparing myself. Eventually you gave me real kingdom responsibility. And I loved it. So I just wanted to tell you today . . . thanks for letting me in the game. See ya." And he hung up.

I'll remember that call for a long time.

Leaders please get this: You and I are at our leadership best when we provide challenging, soul-stirring kingdom opportunities for leaders-in-training; when we stand by these developing leaders and cheer them on; when we help them solve problems and pray for them; and when we coach them on to higher levels of effectiveness. That's leadership at its best.

WHAT KEEPS ME ENERGIZED AS A LEADER

WHAT MOTIVATES ME AS a leader more than anything else is seeing leaders I've helped to develop soaring as leaders in the kingdom. I love seeing people in whom I've invested time and energy bearing fruit, having impact, glorifying God and loving it.

Sue Miller is the kind of person who motivates me to keep developing leaders. Sue, a former public school teacher, joined our staff years ago to lead *Promiseland,* Willow's children's ministry. After raising up hundreds of *Promiseland* volunteers and developing a cutting-edge curriculum, Sue assumed leadership of a worldwide movement dedicated to children's ministry. Several months ago, I attended a session where Sue taught three thousand children's ministry workers from all around the world. I stood in the shadows at the back of the room, reflecting on Sue's development as a leader and bawling my eyes out.

I get equally fired up over people like Jon Rasmussen. He was a businessman in our church who didn't think he had much to offer. But I thought differently. So I spent time with him, trained him, and encouraged him to believe that God had gifted him. Eventually he assumed leadership of a Willow building program involving hundreds of thousands of square feet and tens of millions of dollars. Watching Jon lead effectively and joyfully was one of the most fulfilling experiences of my adult life.

And then there's our programming director, Nancy Beach. I met Nancy when she was a fifteen-year-old high school student just discovering that she had a unique ability to lead. Through the years I've watched her build a community of artists at Willow and then inspire artists worldwide to use their gifts to build the church. I wouldn't have missed this for anything in the world.

What keeps me pumped up as a leader? It's watching an attorney leave his lucrative practice to lead a small-groups revolution here at Willow and around the world. It's watching a tool-and-die maker scale back his company involvement to help revitalize the church in Germany. It's watching a young Harvard business school grad give his life to renewing the church worldwide through leading the Willow Creek Association.

Nothing floats my boat like that. Of course I still enjoy the challenge of doing leadership myself. But the older I get, the more I understand the opportunity and the responsibility of helping other leaders find their niche and reach their full potential.

THE NEXT GENERATION OF EMERGING LEADERS

RECENTLY GOD HAS IMPRESSED on me my connection with the next generation of emerging leaders in a very personal way. After my daughter, Shauna, graduated from college, she felt called by God to work in Student Impact, Willow's high school ministry. Some months ago she and her team met in our home to plan their first retreat for five hundred students. They spent hours planning and praying over how to organize recreational activities, how to structure worship experiences, and how to make the teaching relevant to students.

When the weekend of the retreat came, it was obvious that God had worked. Hundreds of students' lives were changed, commitments were made, and relationships were formed and deepened.

After the retreat, Shauna drove 160 miles around Lake Michigan for the sole purpose of coming to our cottage to tell me all about it. Tears streamed down her face as she described how God had worked. I knew exactly what she had experienced. I remembered clearly what it was like to be a young leader and to realize that you had just been used by God. I remembered clearly what it was like to have something that you planned turn out better than your wildest dreams, because God showed up in a mighty way. I remembered clearly how that could melt a young leader's heart.

To experience God working through my own leadership gift still shakes me to my core from time to time. But to see the same thing happening through my daughter . . . to see her soar . . . to see the next generation of leaders spread their wings and start to fly—that really is about as good as leadership gets.

Whatever challenges our churches face in the years ahead, I hope we can face them with confidence, knowing that we were wise enough to invest in the next generation of leaders. There is nothing that seasoned leaders can do that can have more impact than that. Whatever we do, we must create leadership cultures. We must identify emerging leaders, invest in them, give them kingdom responsibilities, and coach them into effectiveness. Then we can each experience the thrill of watching them soar.

That will be leadership at its very, very best.

CHAPTER SEVEN

Discovering and Developing Your Own Leadership Style

The Key to High-Impact Leading

THE EXPRESSION ON HIS FACE SAID IT ALL. WHEN I PLACED MY HAND on his shoulder and said, "I see leadership qualities in you. You should develop your God-given potential," he replied by wordlessly shaking his head, even as he smiled at the possibility. I could guess the reason for his conflicted response. In his mind, a leader was someone who confidently stood in front of crowds casting vision and motivating the masses, a person born to thrive in the public eye. He simply didn't think he fit the mold.

And he didn't. Not that particular mold anyway. But I had not misread him. He *was* a leader.

Through the years I've learned that leadership actually has many faces. The man in whom I'd spotted leadership potential simply had a different style of leading than the more common leadership type to which he had compared himself. Over time, as his style of leadership fell into sync with an appropriate leadership need in his church, he became a high-impact lay leader.

Different leadership styles are the subject of an insightful book called *A Certain Trumpet* by author Garry Wills. In this book Wills describes different styles of leadership and theorizes that, historically, certain leaders have had unusually high impact because their particular style of leadership meshed perfectly with a specific need in society.

For example, he states that when a certain segment of society needs to break free from a yoke of oppression, a radical leader is called for—a transforming leader.

In American culture, Harriet Tubman was such a leader. As a runaway slave, she became one of the most active guides, or "conductors," for the Underground Railroad. Respectfully known as "Moses," she had great impact because her style of leading met a society's pre-emancipation need for a leader daring enough to embrace the goal of liberation.

What kind of leader best meets the needs of a complex pluralistic democracy like the United States? Wills argues that people like Lee Iacocca or Norman Schwarzkopf—leaders with an autocratic leadership style—would be disastrous. A better fit would be someone who could gradually form consensus across a wide constituent base and eventually form a united coalition. That's why men like Washington, Lincoln, and Roosevelt were such popular and effective leaders; their leadership styles meshed well with the needs of a complex pluralistic society.

Wills asserts that in times of war a military style of leadership works best; hence a Napoleon rises to the top. In times of intense ideological struggle, a nation is best served by an intellectual leader who can help a society think through complicated issues on a collective level. An example of an intellectual leader is Vaclav Havel, the playwright and social activist who, after the collapse of Communism, was elected president of Czechoslovakia and later of the Czech Republic, serving as the moral and ethical force in the country's politics.

Will's fascinating approach to leadership supports an observation I have been making about church leaders for many years. Different leaders often lead with dramatically different styles. As I can discern it, they all have the spiritual gift of leadership, but they express that gift in varied ways.

Additionally, certain leadership styles fit better than others with specific kingdom needs. I am increasingly convinced that highly effective leaders often have impact not only because they are highly gifted but also because their leadership styles mesh perfectly with specific ministry needs. It follows then that discovering and developing unique leadership styles is another major key to leadership effectiveness.

As you read this chapter, I would challenge you to try to identify your leadership style and the styles of other leaders on your team. Then consider how you and your team members might have even greater impact by matching your particular styles with specific leadership needs in your church.

1. THE VISIONARY LEADERSHIP STYLE

WHAT DISTINGUISHES THE VISIONARY leader is that he or she has a crystal clear picture in mind of what the future could hold. Such a leader casts powerful visions and has indefatigable enthusiasm for turning those visions into reality.

Visionary leaders shamelessly appeal to anybody and everybody to get on board with their vision. They talk about it, write about, and burn white-hot for it themselves. They are idealistic, faith-filled leaders who wholeheartedly believe that if they cast their vision clearly enough and often enough *it will become reality.* They are not easily discouraged or deterred. People who tell them it can't be done just fuel the fire of their spirit. They respond to opposition by digging in their heels and raising their voices even louder. Put them in front of the troops and they will splash vision all over them.

Visionary leaders may or may not have the natural ability to form teams, align talents, set goals, or manage progress toward the achievement of the vision. To be effective over the long haul they will either have to find other people who can help them or they will have to work very hard to develop the skills that don't come naturally to them. But this one thing is sure: they carry the vision, they cast the vision, they draw people into it, and they'll die trying to fulfill it.

Do you know anybody with the visionary style of leadership? Is it you or someone on your team?

2. THE DIRECTIONAL LEADERSHIP STYLE

THE DIRECTIONAL STYLE OF leadership doesn't get much press, but it is exceedingly important. The strength of this leader is his or her uncanny, God-given ability to choose the right path for an organization as it approaches a critical intersection.

What do I mean by this?

A critical intersection is that point when an organization, a department, or a church starts asking, "Should we stay the course or is it time for wholesale change? Should we focus on growth or on consolidation? Should we start new ministries or deepen and improve existing ones? Should we build a new facility, renovate the old one, or relocate? Should we start a contemporary service or update our traditional service? Should we start a Gen X ministry or work harder to integrate younger attendees into our existing ministries? Should we steer the organization fifteen degrees to either side of the course we're presently taking? Is it time for some fresh staff or can we keep on dancing with those who brought us here? Which course should we take?"

These are directional issues and they are huge, so huge that they often immobilize a church or sub-ministry. But a leader with a directional style is able to sort through all the options. He or she can carefully assess the values of the organization, the mission, the strengths, the weaknesses, the resources, the personnel, and the openness to change. With remarkable wisdom, the directional leader points the church or sub-ministry in the right direction.

This style of leadership is extremely important because mistakes at key intersections can wreck organizations. In the Old Testament, shortly after Solomon's death, his son Rehoboam became king. Almost immediately the new king encountered his first critical intersection. Representatives of the people in his kingdom came to him requesting that their workloads be reduced. Solomon had worked the people to the point of utter exhaustion. Would Rehoboam do the same?

When Rehoboam consulted with his counselors, he received mixed advice. While older counselors advised him to ease up, the younger ones countered with, "Load them up!" Unfortunately he listened to the younger voices and made the wrong call at a critical intersection. It destroyed the kingdom.

One intersection. One call. But so much can hang in the balance for the church or ministry at these critical points.

Directional leaders may or may not have high profile in an organization. They may or may not be able to stand up in front of people and excel at public leadership. But their unique style makes an exceedingly important contribution to the whole.

There are two individuals on our board of directors with whom I consult privately before I make a move at any critical intersection. While I value the input of every board member, I feel very uncomfortable moving ahead on any important issues unless these two board members give me a green light. Twice during the early years of my leadership, before I understood the contribution of this style of leadership, I chose to go against the judgment of these two men. Both times, Willow paid dearly. I have long since learned to defer to seasoned directional leaders.

Interestingly, neither of these directional leaders feels comfortable speaking publicly. Neither exhibits many other signs of leadership. But they are directional monsters, two of the secret heroes of Willow.

3. THE STRATEGIC LEADERSHIP STYLE

STRATEGIC LEADERS HAVE THE God-given ability to take an exciting vision and break it down into a series of sequential, achievable steps. This gift of leadership allows an organization to march intentionally toward the actualization of its mission.

Visions excite people. They inspire people. They compel people into action. But unless people eventually see progress toward the fulfillment of the vision they will conclude that the vision caster is just a dreamer blowing smoke, and their morale will plummet.

Strategically oriented leaders form a game plan that everybody can understand and participate in. Then they challenge team members to "work the plan." They say, "Don't go off on tangents. Don't get distracted. Just put one foot in front of the other according to the plan. Come to work and do what needs to be done today to take the first step. Then tomorrow take the next step, then the next. Stay with the plan and you'll reach the goal." And that's what happens under a strategic leader: the game plan eventually leads to the actualization of the vision.

A strategic leader will also strive to bring the various subgroups of an organization into alignment so that all the organization's energy will be focused toward realizing the vision.

As I mentioned earlier, in the mid nineties I felt the need to develop a five-year strategic plan for Willow. Yet I knew I wasn't the leader to quarterback that effort. Why? I'm not strong enough as a strategist. So I asked my Executive Pastor, Greg Hawkins, to head up that effort because he's the strongest strategic leader on our team. Not only did Greg develop and present the plan, but he managed it to completion as well. No one on our team was better suited to play that role.

Every church and every organization needs someone who provides this critical strategic component to the leadership team.

4. THE MANAGING LEADERSHIP STYLE

ACCORDING TO SOME LEADERSHIP literature, the term "managing leader" is an oxymoron. That's because some leadership experts draw careful distinctions between what managers do and what leaders do. It is often said that "leaders do right things, while managers do things right." I agree with certain distinctions commonly drawn between managers and leaders. But when referring to a managing leadership style, I'm describing a leader who has the ability to organize people, processes, and resources to achieve a mission.

The managing leader salivates at the thought of bringing order out of chaos. He or she finds deep satisfaction in monitoring and fine-tuning a process, and motivates team members by establishing appropriate mile markers on the road to the destination.

It's surprising how many visionary leaders are inept at managing people, processes, and money. It's also surprising how many directional and strategic leaders are incapable of actually putting the players and plans and resources in place to achieve the goals of the organization. Around the leadership circles at Willow, I often say, "Sooner or later someone's going to have to manage all of this stuff!" Because we've always had an abundance of visionary, directional, and strategic leaders and a shortage of managing leaders, we have a tendency to come up with lots of ideas that nobody has the capacity or inclination to carry out.

Managing leaders seldom captivate attention as do those who give the inspiring vision talks or make the critical decisions or put the strategic plans in place. But in the day-to-day operational world, someone has to manage people and progress to move the organization toward its goals.

I have a growing appreciation for managing leaders. These days, I'm on the constant lookout for people who can make this kind of leadership contribution both to the church and to the Willow Creek Association.

I think Joseph in the Old Testament was an excellent managing leader. Nehemiah was one as well. Both of these men effectively organized and accomplished huge tasks.

5. THE MOTIVATIONAL LEADERSHIP STYLE

LEADERS WITH THE MOTIVATIONAL style are the modern day Vince Lombardis. They have that God-given ability to keep their teammates fired up. They are on the constant lookout for "sagging shoulders and dull eyes," and they move quickly to inject the right kind of inspiration into those who need it most. They have a keen sense about who needs public recognition and who needs just a private word of encouragement. They seem to know exactly when a particular team member would get a necessary boost from a day off, an office move, a title change, or a training opportunity.

Some leaders view the motivational approach as a lightweight style of leadership. But it's a huge mistake to underestimate the value of this style. As a team member I'd be glad to make do with a lower-voltage vision caster, an occasional bad call at an intersection, or a periodic lapse of managerial effectiveness, if the leader I reported to would consistently fire me up, call out my best, cheer on my progress, celebrate my accomplishments, and tell me I was important to the cause.

I would follow a leader like that to the grave!

Motivational leaders realize that even our best teammates get tired out and lose focus. Sometimes our most dependable colleagues experience mission drift or start to wonder if what they're doing really matters to God or anybody else.

Motivational leaders don't get bitter or vengeful when morale sinks. They view it as an opportunity to dream of new ways to inspire and lift the spirits of everyone on the team.

Jesus consistently motivated his disciples. He changed Simon's name and honored him as Peter, the rock upon which he would build his church. He motivated his followers with promises of reward in this life and in the next. He planned getaways and retreats.

Do you know what many teammates desire more than anything else? An hour or two to spend with their leader when there is no pressing agenda on the flip chart. An occasional opportunity to interact with their leader as a fellow human being rather than as a worker under his or her command. Jesus often took his disciples and escaped from ministry concerns. He'd say, "Now is not the time to take a hill. It's time to sleep at the bottom of one. So let's go." Or, "This would be a nice evening for just hanging out together. Let's go fishing and then come back and cook supper on the beach." Can you imagine how much the disciples cherished those times?

Jesus also motivated his disciples by the way he trained them. After mentoring them he sent them out two-by-two to do ministry. When they returned he reviewed what they had experienced and provided feedback for them. Then he would say something like this: "I want to call you friends. I know this isn't the traditional, impersonal, corporate arrangement, but this is the way I want it. Think of us as family." Imagine the motivational power of Jesus' gift of friendship.

John Maxwell, president of Injoy, is one of the most effective motivational leaders I've ever known. My wife kids me when John and I do conferences together on the road. She says, "Oh no! You're going to come back on an adrenaline rush." And when I call her at night from the hotel, she always asks, "So, just how much fun did you two have today?"

And I'm always happy to report, "Way too much, Lynne. Illegal amounts." The fun comes, in part, from how much we inspire each other.

As I'm preparing to speak at a conference, John sometimes whispers to me, "This is going to be the best talk you have ever given in your life." Or he'll pray for me, "Oh God, take Bill to a whole new level this morning." Often I will pray a similar prayer for him.

On one occasion John took a unique motivational approach. I was falling ill on one of our trips together, fighting a high fever and nausea. I had found a couch in a back room of the conference center and had collapsed on it, wishing I could spend the next day and a half there. But both John and I felt that the talk I was scheduled to deliver was important for everyone to hear. Knowing my inability to back off from a challenge, John knelt by the couch and whispered, "I think you're much too sick to handle this final talk . . . But don't worry, I can handle it for you . . . You just snuggle down under those blankets and suck your thumb . . . I'll patch together a talk and bail you out."

My response was immediate. "Get out of my way. I'll fall over and die before I let you do that!"

John's a tremendous motivator—twisted at times—but a wonderful motivational leader just the same.

If you're that kind of leader, don't ever underestimate what you bring to your team. God has given you a special ability. Use it! For what it's worth, I'd sign up for your team any day.

6. THE SHEPHERDING LEADERSHIP STYLE

THE SHEPHERDING LEADER IS a man or a woman who builds a team slowly, loves team members deeply, nurtures them gently, supports them consistently, listens to them patiently, and prays for them diligently. This kind of leader draws team members into such a rich community experience that their hearts begin to overflow with good will that energizes them for achieving their mission.

While visionary leaders tend to attract people because of the compelling nature of their cause, shepherding leaders tend to draw people together almost regardless of their cause. In other words, shepherding leaders tend to shepherd and nurture a group of folks so thoroughly, so deeply, that when it comes to the cause, teammates are often heard to say, "The cause doesn't matter all that much. If it's a God-honoring mission that we can do together, count me in. As long as we can stay in community and keep our shepherd, we'll do it."

Under a shepherding leader the range of vision can be very broad. What really matters are the community dynamics.

In 2 Samuel 23 we read that David, at the beginning of his leadership career, drew together a group of lonely and disaffected followers. Then he built into them deeply and shepherded them lovingly. One night, during a period of intense struggle with their Philistine enemies, David happened to mention that he was thirsty and longed for water from the wells of Bethlehem. In response to David's longing, and unknown to him, three members of his team crept behind enemy lines, risking their lives, to bring David water from Bethlehem's wells. The deep care David's teammates had received from him made them want to return love and service back to him.

When they presented the water to David, he was extremely moved, realizing that the men had risked their lives for his sake. He was so moved, in fact, that he refused to drink it. "Far be it from me, O Lord, to do this," he said (vs. 17). In other words, "I can't drink water that men risked their lives for!" Instead, the Bible tells us that David "poured it out before the Lord" (vs. 16). I can't help but think that in this worship offering David was celebrating not only the greatness of his God but also the love of his team.

Leaders must remember that although there are many cause-driven people who are waiting to be drawn into a mission by a visionary leader, there are also plenty of community starved people who need to be welcomed onto a team where they can be nurtured and loved. Only then will they be motivated to answer the call of a cause. Without tender care they will hold back, but if shepherded lovingly they will joyfully pursue almost any kingdom purpose with loyal dedication.

Do you know any shepherding leaders? Respect what they bring to the kingdom. They may not excel at casting visions or putting strategic plans in place, but their unique ability to shepherd people positions them to make a huge kingdom difference.

7. THE TEAM-BUILDING LEADERSHIP STYLE

THE TEAM-BUILDING LEADER knows the vision and understands how to achieve it, but realizes it will take a team of leaders and workers to accomplish the goal. Team-builders have a supernatural insight into people that allows them to successfully find and develop the right people with the right abilities, the right character, and the right chemistry with other team members. Then good team-builders know how to put these people in the right positions for the right reasons, thus freeing them to produce the right results.

When the appropriate people have been placed in appropriate positions, the team-building leader says to the appointed team, "You know what we're trying to do. You know what part of the mission you're responsible for. You know what part the rest of us around the circle are responsible for. So—head out! Get on with it! Work hard in your department. Communicate with your co-laborers. Create action. Get the job done!"

The difference between the shepherding leader and the team-building leader is that the team-builder is driven more by a clear understanding of the vision than by the desire to nurture and build community. Of course, building teams always involves building community, but the unique strength of team-building leaders is that they have a stranglehold on the strategy and an acute insight into people that allows them to make precise placements of personnel into critical leadership roles.

Leaders gifted as team-builders may or may not be skilled at managing their teams. In fact, many of them reason that management isn't all that critical anyway; if the right people are in the right slots doing the right things for the right reasons, these people will accomplish their goals whether or not there is someone looking over their shoulders.

When Phil Jackson coached the Chicago Bulls basketball team during their glory years, he demonstrated this leadership style. He selected the right people for specific roles and made his expectations clear: "Michael Jordan, you score thirty or forty points a game and lead and inspire your teammates. Dennis Rodman, you get twenty rebounds a game and mess with the opposition's minds. (And after the game, go dress in drag and mess with everybody's minds.) Scottie Pippen, you score your fifteen points, get ten rebounds, and play huge defense. Luke Longley, you just drape yourself over their big guy. Ron Harper, you stop their best shooter, then get the ball to Michael and Scottie. Tony Kukoc, you come off the bench and spark the team."

Finding the right people to do the right things consistent with their best skills is the hallmark of the team-building leadership style.

While I have been reluctant to mention my own leadership styles I suspect it has become obvious by now that I love to build teams. Throughout my leadership life I have been motivated by the goal of putting together a kingdom dream team. As I mentioned earlier, part of what brings me tremendous joy and almost unlimited energy at this point in my life is that I know I am in the midst of realizing that dream.

The communicators who share teaching responsibilities with me at Willow are phenomenal. Our music, drama, and dance teams are amazing. Willow's management team, board of directors, and elders, along with the board and senior leadership team for the Willow Creek Association—they are all kingdom dream teams!

While I was writing this chapter in a Burger King in South Haven, Michigan, tears streamed down my cheeks, and I thought, *There is nothing like drawing together the right people and putting them in the right positions. There is nothing like forming a kingdom dream team and watching it soar to higher and higher levels of impact.* I can't deny it; the heart of a team-builder beats in my chest. Maybe it beats in yours too.

8. THE ENTREPRENEURIAL LEADERSHIP STYLE

THE ENTREPRENEURIAL LEADERSHIP STYLE has a unique twist. Entrepreneurial leaders may possess any of the other leadership styles, but what distinguishes these leaders from the others is that they function optimally in start-up mode. If these leaders can't regularly give birth to something new they begin to lose energy. Once a venture is up and operational, once the effort requires steady ongoing management, once things get complicated and require endless discussions about policies, systems, and controls, then most entrepreneurial leaders lose enthusiasm, focus, and sometimes even confidence.

At that point they start peeking over the fence and wondering if it might be time to start something new. They may feel terribly guilty at the thought of leaving the ministry, organization, or department they started, but eventually they have to face the truth: if they can't give birth to something brand new every few years, something inside of them starts to die.

That's just their style. And it's important in the kingdom.

I believe the apostle Paul was an entrepreneurial leader. He pioneered and built churches in areas where the name of Christ was not yet known. After launching these churches he turned them over to other people who could run them, so that he could move on—without apology. He may not have described himself with these exact words, but he obviously knew how he was gifted and how he could most optimally serve the kingdom.

There are entrepreneurial leaders at Willow who start ministries, grow them up for awhile, and then announce that it's time for someone else to take them over. Next thing we know, these same leaders are starting new ministries, and we are scrambling to find people to take over these programs as well. At times I have had to deliver ultimatums, "No more starting stuff!" We have actually had to invite a few leaders off our staff because they could not resist the temptation to start new ministries. "Go someplace else and start things," we finally had to tell them. "We need fifteen managing leaders to stabilize and grow the ministries you've already started. The last thing we need right now is another half-grown ministry!"

But how the kingdom would be diminished if entrepreneurial leaders stopped dreaming new dreams and starting new ventures.

9. THE REENGINEERING LEADERSHIP STYLE

WHILE ENTREPRENEURIAL LEADERS LOVE to start new endeavors, reengineering leaders are at their best in turn-around environments. These leaders are gifted by God to thrive on the challenge of taking a troubled situation—a team that has lost its vision, a ministry where people are in wrong positions, a department trying to move forward without a strategy—and turning it around. This leader says, "This is my lucky day. I get to start reengineering this mess."

These leaders enthusiastically dig in to uncover the original mission and the cause of the mission drift. They reevaluate personnel, strategy, and values. They repeatedly meet with team members to help them figure out where the "old" went wrong and what the "new" should look like. Then they prod team members on to action.

Reengineering leaders love to patch up, tune up, and revitalize hurting departments or organizations. But when everything is back on track and operating smoothly, these leaders may or may not be motivated to stay engaged. Some of them are content to stick around and enjoy the fruits of their labors, but many prefer to find another department or organization that needs to be overhauled. When they find one they start salivating. "Would you look at that kingdom train wreck?" they say. "If I could get my hands on all that twisted metal, I know I could turn it into something great for God."

I wasn't aware of this leadership style until about fifteen years into my leadership at Willow. At that point, we were facing a huge challenge. After growing at a high rate for a decade and a half, all our systems seemed to be falling apart at once. The analogy we used to describe our situation at that time was that we had unknowingly built a twenty-story building on a ten-story foundation. The building had held up for a while, but now, before our eyes, the infrastructure was starting to give way. One sub-ministry after the next was beginning to crumble.

At this time a very gifted leader joined our staff. The more I got to know him the more I liked him. The only problem was that he didn't want to start anything, shepherd anything, or manage anything long-term. But I strongly sensed that the guy was a leader. So not knowing how else to use him, we assigned him to help reorganize some very messy departments. Ten years later, we stood in awe at what this individual had accomplished in rebuilding some of Willow's most vital ministries—pastoral care, children's ministry, programming, operations, and many others. This man became a legend around Willow without ever starting a single ministry or leading anything long-term. We say, "Yea, God!" every time we see him walk the hallways of Willow, knowing that his ability to reengineer rescued some of our most strategic ministries from untimely deaths.

I believe that God has placed reengineering leaders in every church. It's your job and mine to find them and put them to work.

10. THE BRIDGE-BUILDING LEADERSHIP STYLE

THOUGH THERE ARE ADDITIONAL leadership styles that could be mentioned, for the purposes of this book I'd like to end with the bridge-building style. While author Garry Wills calls this the electoral or political style, I call it the bridge-building style because I am referring to it outside of a political framework.

Bridge-building leaders make important contributions to large organizations such as parachurch ministries, denominations, and educational institutions because they have the unique ability to bring together under a single leadership umbrella a wide range of constituent groups. This enables a complex organization to stay focused on a single mission.

The unique gift that bridge-building leaders bring to this feat is enormous flexibility. They are diplomats who possess a supernaturally inspired ability to compromise and negotiate. They are specially gifted to listen, understand, and think outside of the box. But above everything else, bridge-builders love the challenge of relating to diverse groups of people.

In start-up ventures leaders are usually surrounded by family members and close friends who share their exciting new vision. All goes well until that little start-up group doubles or triples in size. New people bring new leadership challenges. How do all these new people fit into the original group? What happens when the leadership team has to be divided? How do you maintain optimal group dynamics? How does the point leader relate to all these people?

Now imagine leading a megachurch or large parachurch organization made up of scores of well-defined constituencies. Many of these special interest groups care little about the overall vision of the umbrella ministry. They simply want to make sure that their particular concerns are attended to.

I talked to a pastor recently who was pulling out what few strands of hair he had left. "I'm dying," he said. "The choir wants new designer robes and the youth group wants a new gymnasium. The missions department wants to give another million dollars away and the children's ministry wants more classrooms. The production people want new equipment and the seniors want large print hymnals. The Gen X-ers want to turn the board room into a cappuccino bar and the junior high department wants a skateboard park."

The variety of those requests and the velocity at which they were coming overwhelmed him. He had begun to view each of those sub-ministries as the enemy. The subtext of his complaint was, "I can't live my life like this. I can't stand being pulled in so many directions."

As I listened to him I realized that this man was not built to head up an organization of that complexity. Leading in such an environment would never energize him; most likely, it would continue to be a defeating experience. To maximize his leadership potential he would probably have to move to a less complex situation.

In contrast, bridge-building leaders are most energized when facing the challenge of drawing together and meeting the needs of varied constituents. These leaders would joyfully meet privately with the heads of various sub-ministries to understand their passions and their goals. After building relationships of trust, the bridge-builders would try to refine the vision of each sub-leader, negotiating with them until their goals were working in harmony with the overall vision and mission of the larger organization.

The goal of a bridge-building leader is to become an effective advocate for each constituent group, ultimately uniting and focusing the efforts of all the groups in such a way that it creates a win-win situation for everyone involved. The bridge-builder does this by helping each group develop a healthier perspective and realize that they can meet the needs of their sub-ministry *and* contribute to the achievement of the overall mission as well.

Dealing with complexity is a bridge-building leader's forte. Large organizations must be led by such leaders.

FOUR STEPS IN DISCOVERING AND DEVELOPING YOUR LEADERSHIP STYLE

THE FIRST STEP IN identifying your own leadership style is to review the style descriptions offered in this chapter. You may find yourself resonating with one style of leadership or with several.

After you've identified your style or styles, share your discovery with people who are familiar with your leadership. Ask them if they agree with your conclusion. Self-assessment can be confusing, so it's important to seek input from other people.

Second, you must determine whether or not your style fits your current leadership situation. This can be a delicate and potentially painful process, but it is extremely important to discern whether or not your leadership strengths actually fit the role you are being expected to fill. For example, if you are an entrepreneurial leader in a hundred-year-old church that is not interested in starting anything new *ever,* you will probably end up blowing the place apart. If you're a managing leader in an organization that is dying for lack of vision, you will eventually find yourself with nothing left to lead. In either case, you have some difficult decisions to make.

But know this: There are undoubtedly many situations where your leadership style would sync perfectly with the given needs. Your challenge is to determine whether or not you're in that kind of situation now.

The third step is to determine the leadership style of each person on your team. Do this together by reading the leadership style descriptions and circling where each person is high and low. There are two reasons why you need to understand each team member's leadership style. First, it helps you make sure that each team member is matched with the leadership need that allows him or her to have the greatest impact. Second, it allows you to determine what leadership function is lacking on your team and what style of leader you should add next, either as a permanent staff member or as a guest contributor.

I believe there are some leadership styles without which an organization cannot survive, and I am convinced that many organizations suffer because they aren't aware of this. Every organization, be it a church, college, university, hospital, or business, needs a visionary leader who can communicate a clear vision in a compelling way. Organizations that aren't sustained by a captivating vision eventually die.

Every organization also needs a workable strategy. If there's nobody on your team who can put together a step-by-step plan for turning vision into reality, then you had better find a strategic leader willing to join you or hire a consultant who can assist you. You won't move forward without someone who can consistently offer expertise in this area.

You may think your team can function fine without someone contributing motivational or shepherding strengths, but think again. Every team needs someone who is gifted in lifting the human spirit.

The final step is to commit yourself not only to developing your strongest leadership style but also to growing in the areas in which you are weak. I know there is debate on this. Some experts say, "Forget your weaknesses, just concentrate on your strengths." But I disagree.

Here's why: No matter how strong leaders are in their particular leadership style, totally overlooking the areas in which they are weak will eventually compromise their ability to lead.

For instance, I am low on the managing style. Thankfully I am able to delegate most of the management responsibilities at Willow. Still, there are about a dozen people who report to me. I have to manage those twelve people with some degree of skill. If I don't, they start working at cross-purposes and end up confused and discouraged. Eventually relationships begin to suffer. So for the good of the church, I need to take responsibility for improving my managing skills regardless of my preferred leadership style.

Another example: If you are a point leader who is low on the motivational style, you would serve your team members well by learning how to motivate and inspire. Why? Because they deserve it. No matter how many other people pump them up in other settings, they need to receive a certain amount of "atta boys" and "atta girls" directly from you.

So, here again are my suggestions for meshing leadership styles with organizational needs in order to lead with high impact.

1. Identify your leadership style or styles.
2. Determine if your style fits your current leadership situation.
3. Identify the leadership style of each member on your team. Make sure each person is matched up with the right leader-

ship need and determine if there are leadership gaps on your team that need to be filled
4. Commit yourself both to developing your strong leadership styles *and* growing in your weaker leadership styles.

I urge you to act on these suggestions. When leaders are optimally positioned so that their leadership strengths mesh perfectly with the specific needs of a church or an organization they can have huge impact. Under their leadership the troops can be mobilized, the mission can be achieved, and the kingdom can move forward like never before.

CHAPTER EIGHT

A Leader's Sixth Sense

The Sources of Decision Making

A FEW YEARS AGO A MOVIE CALLED *THE SIXTH SENSE* BECAME A worldwide box office smash. The story revolved around a young boy who had the mysterious capacity to see and perceive what other people could not. The boy's most memorable and now famous line was, "I see dead people." A pastor said to me, "Big deal. I see that at every deacon's meeting." But in the movie it was decidedly eerie.

Usually when people talk about a *sixth sense,* they're referring to a kind of knowing that is intuitive and perceptive beyond what is normal.

For example, I know a woman whose leadership compass often seems to work better than anyone else's in the room. Periodically her team wrestles with the direction the organization needs to take in the future. Everything looks murky and confusing. Then this human compass, who has been listening quietly the whole time, suggests a certain course of action. Team members ponder her idea for a moment or two, then heads begin to nod positively. "That's it. Of course, that's it!" Inside they're thinking, *How does she do that? Where does she get those ideas? What does she have that the rest of us don't have?*

I know leaders who seem able to perceive the future. It's as though they can fast forward the video that the rest of us are watching at normal speed. They seem to have a special ability to sense the implications of current decisions on future reality.

Some leaders seem to be uniquely gifted to spot the one glittering diamond of opportunity buried in a coal mine of problems. Everyone else is overwhelmed and discouraged, but these leaders are undaunted; they see what no one else can see—potential in the midst of disaster.

Other leaders can discern leadership potential in people whom most of us would write off. It appears that they're placing their bet on a sure loser, but in the end they're proven right. We all watch as the person they selected soars in a leadership role.

How do we explain this uncanny ability that some leaders have? Does it come automatically with the spiritual gift of leadership? Does it show up one day out of nowhere? Do some leaders really have heightened intuition? Or do all leaders have it equally? Can it be developed?

Let me explain what prompted my thinking about the intuitive side of leadership. I was in a staff meeting in which a number of important decisions had to be made. Other staff members were eagerly awaiting these decisions so that they could press ahead with their ministries. Deadlines were approaching. Printing schedules were pressing.

Despite the high stakes attached to some of these decisions, none of them seemed particularly difficult for me to make. I simply listened to each proposal and asked for input from my trusted advisors and colleagues who sat around the table. Throughout the meeting I silently prayed for the Holy Spirit to give me wisdom, as James 1:5 instructs us to do. Then, near the end of the meeting, I made what I felt were the appropriate decisions.

After the meeting a long-term staff member elbowed me in the ribs and joked, "That's just recreation to you, isn't it? I've watched you do this for years, and it's just not fair. You make it look so easy." As he started to leave, he turned back, smiled, and said, "And what really makes me sick is how often you are right!"

I said, "No big deal. Even a broken clock is right twice a day." But that conversation got me thinking about a leader's decision-making process. How intuitive is it, really?

EXPLORING MY OWN DECISION-MAKING PROCESS

FOR THE NEXT THIRTY days, I tried an experiment that I'd never tried before. I kept a pad of paper with me, and every time I made a leadership decision—large or small, carefully thought through or made reflexively—I jotted the decision down on that pad.

When the thirty days were over, I evaluated each and every decision. I wanted to determine what factors informed my decision-making process. I wanted to try to understand this rumored "sixth sense" of leaders.

Let me give you my conclusion first, then I'll unpack it. I believe that spiritually gifted leaders construct, over time, a value system and experience base that wisely informs each subsequent decision they make. As they diligently add to this personal database year after year, they automatically increase their leadership batting averages. So it's not some mysterious sixth sense or supernatural phenomenon that gives effective leaders unusual insight and wisdom. Rather, their ability to see what others miss is the fairly predictable result of embracing the right values and letting those values inform their perceptions of reality and the choices they make based on those perceptions.

Before this thirty-day experiment, I hadn't thought much about the sources that informed my decision making. But after reflecting on what drove each decision of the previous month, I could see that most of my decisions were informed by four distinct data sources.

MY FIRST DATA SOURCE: WHAT I BELIEVE

LET ME USE AN illustration to explain how the "What-I-believe" data source works. One decision that landed on my desk during that thirty-day period involved one of the international offices of the WCA. A senior leader in that affiliate had just left our employment to work elsewhere, but before he left he had made some questionable financial commitments involving enough money for the matter to reach my desk.

A number of people from the business community were showing up at the affiliate office asking to be paid for work they had been contracted to do. The leader who had recently left the office claimed that he had made all those payments, but there were no records to substantiate his claim. I was asked to decide what to do in this situation. I answered immediately. "Pay them. Pay all of them. Pay whatever they ask." I didn't spend three seconds pondering that decision. I never even bothered to say a prayer. That decision was a no-brainer.

Being a Dutchman, I find parting with any money to be an emotional experience; if there's any question about whether I ought to be parting with it, it's even worse. Still, this decision was easy because of certain convictions I hold. These are the "what-I-believe" convictions that operate beneath the surface of my leadership. They inform my decision-making process every day.

Can I share with you a few of these convictions?

1. If I Honor God In Everything, He Will Honor Me

I believe that if I do my best to honor God in everything I do, he will honor my leadership, and he will honor the ministry he has entrusted to my care. This is not a wall plaque nicety to me. It's not just the spiritually correct thing to write to Christian leaders. This is a bedrock, unshakable, to-the-core-of-my-being belief that I carry with me wherever I go.

I really do believe that the sovereign God will pour out his divine blessing and come to the rescue of any leader who consistently attempts to honor God in everything.

I believe the converse is true as well. I believe that if we dishonor God by taking shortcuts in our lives or our ministries or by compromising our character or by refusing to obey the Spirit's promptings, then we should not expect to receive help from heaven. In his grace, God might still grant his favor, but we shouldn't count on it.

I've learned over the years that I truly need help from heaven to do what I do. I'm not a good enough leader to lead what has been entrusted to me without divine intervention. I desperately need God's blessing. So whenever I have to make a decision I will make the choice that I believe honors God the most.

How did this impact my decision to pay the workers? I believed that God's reputation was at stake in how we responded to the claims of the business community. Better for us to risk the possibility of paying the workers twice than risk the possibility of not giving them their due.

2. People Matter

I think it's safe to say that God has only one true treasure in his whole cosmos, and that's people. So the second bedrock belief that informs my decision-making is that people matter to God.

Scripture teaches that if we show sensitivity and deference to what God treasures most in this world—people—then he will in turn show mercy and deference to us (1 Samuel 2:30b; Matthew 22:37–39). To the core of my being I believe that if I honor people and treat them graciously, God will show favor to me and to those I lead.

So whenever there's a human component to a decision that comes my way, my antenna goes way up. When I know that someone's welfare hangs in the balance, I work overtime to get that decision right. I have told our elders and board members that if I am going to err, I'd rather err on the side of being gracious to people. I'd much rather have to stand before God someday and take my lumps for being too merciful than for being too harsh.

3. The Local Church Is the Hope of the World

As you may have gathered by now, this third bedrock belief is my favorite mantra. I believe to the core of my being that the local church is the hope of the world.

Most people mistakenly assume that I'm pretty intense about everything. But I'm not. Ask my closest friends. There are a lot of things I don't get amped up about. I don't care particularly what restaurants I go to or what evening activities I engage in. I'm not very interested in clothes or cars or home furnishings or being "socially proper." I don't put a lot of thought or energy into politics or into who will win the World Series.

But if you accuse me of being intense about the Church, then I stand guilty as charged. I freely admit that I take very seriously any decision that has major implications for the future health, unity, or effectiveness of Willow, or increasingly of the capital-C church. Like the favorite expression of a crewmember on my boat, "I'm on that like a rat on a Cheeto!" I'd do almost anything to make sure that the church is well led and that decisions made on her behalf are made with care and wisdom.

Side Note: If You're Going to Let Anything Slide . . .

Please allow me a brief tangent.

I have a hard time understanding how some Christian business people can agonize so deeply over corporate decisions—how they can hold endless strategy meetings, hire expensive consultants, and go to bed with five-year forecasts—and yet when it comes to decisions that impact the church they attend, those same people are passive and indifferent. They could be offering their expertise to the church as board members, elders, or special project chairmen. The high-impact volunteer opportunities in most churches are unlimited, but these talented, gifted, competent men and women would rather devote every bit of their time, energy, and expertise to the corporate world. I don't get it and I probably never will.

Sometimes I want to say to these Christian folks, "Listen! What you're so exercised about at work, it's only money. It's not worth all the angst it's producing in you. It's not worth lying awake at night getting ulcers. It's not like it has eternal impact. Let's keep a little perspective!"

The local church is the hope of the world because it stewards the only message that can impact a person's eternal destiny. If we really believe that, how can we not want to put our best decision-making ability to work in the local church body to which God has called us, whether we're pastors or businesspersons?

Sometimes a newer board member will call me the day of a board meeting and ask what is on the agenda that night. This is usually code for, "Things are pretty intense at work. I am thinking of skipping the board meeting tonight."

While I am always concerned about the marketplace challenges of our board members—I grew up in the home of a businessman and I genuinely enjoy the hours I've spent discussing work-related issues with my board members—the veterans don't bother calling me about skipping a board meeting. They know my response will be something along the lines of, "I'm sorry things are so tense at work. Let's pray right now about the challenges you're facing. But don't forget that thousands of Willow Creekers need you to show up tonight, fresh, prayed up, and ready to give your best energy and creativity to the challenges that affect the future of the church."

I don't believe my thinking on this issue will ever change. When it comes to making decisions for the church, there is too much at stake to take it lightly.

Okay, now we can get back to the main topic.

WHAT ARE YOUR BEDROCK BELIEFS?

DO YOU KNOW THE core convictions that inform your decision making? When I was trying to get at the root of my core beliefs, I thought I had them right on the tip of my tongue. But I didn't. I had to put my feet up on my desk and journal and pray for several hours before I could unpack the deep convictions that inform my decision making. For review purposes, I'll list them again.

1. Honor God in everything and he'll honor you.
2. People matter to God.
3. The local church is the hope of the world.

It's quite possible I could dig up a fourth, fifth, or sixth belief if I kept the shovel going, but most leaders will do well to identify their top three core beliefs.

But be careful of faulty belief systems. Make sure your convictions are biblical. If not they may be hazardous to your decision-making health.

Remember the leader in Luke 18? In this parable Jesus describes an unjust judge who is harassing a woman. We're told in verse 2 that this leader had "no fear of God and no respect of people." In other words, he didn't worry about honoring God in his daily life. He simply said, "I'll make whatever decisions favor me. How God feels about it is of no concern to me whatsoever." Beyond that he also had no respect for people. "So what if people matter to God. They don't matter to me."

His decisions were informed by a faulty belief system that led to all kinds of corruption. What you believe to be true in the core of your being will influence the decisions you make throughout your leadership life.

If you've been making some poor decisions, if you're creating chaos in your church, at work, or in your family, take a time out and ask: What is going on here? What belief system is informing these bad decisions? Maybe it's time to rebuild the core convictions of your life.

MY SECOND DATA SOURCE: WHAT I KNOW OTHER LEADERS WOULD DO

I WAS SOMEWHAT SURPRISED to discover a second data source influencing me. As I evaluated the decisions I made during those thirty days, I was fascinated by how often my decisions were informed by what I knew other leaders I respected would do if they were facing that particular decision.

These "other leaders" are men and women who I consider to be wiser, more gifted, or more experienced than I am. Some of these veteran leaders are people I know well; they are close personal friends and mentors I've spent a lot of time with. But interestingly some of the leaders who were impacting my decisions during that thirty-day period were people I'd never even met. They've mentored me at a distance through their talks, tapes, or books.

During this period of reflection, I listed the kinds of decisions that landed on my desk and then matched them with the mentor who addressed that kind of decision-making. This was a fascinating exercise.

CONSULTING A RISK-ASSESSMENT MENTOR

OFTEN MY COLLEAGUES ASK for my input on decisions that involve a significant downside risk. Because there's the potential of a big upside gain, they don't want to dismiss the idea, but the downside risk has them paralyzed. So they come to me.

The mentor who impacts me the most when I'm assessing risk is my dad. Although he has been dead for almost twenty-five years, his leadership still powerfully affects my decision making. My father was what I would call a calculated risk-taker, and he was one of the most gifted ones I've ever known.

There are all kinds of risk-takers. On one end of the spectrum are the extravagant risk-takers, the kind who bet the farm repeatedly. They usually end up losing the farm. At the other extreme are leaders who are risk-averse; they wouldn't take a risk if their life depended on it.

My dad was not like either of those extremes. He provided steady, consistent oversight of his core businesses, but he wasn't opposed to taking an occasional risk. He used to say to me as I was growing up, "Billy, if you don't take a flyer once in a while, you'll never learn anything new, and life will get very boring."

When pilots take a new aircraft for a test flight, they are "taking a flyer." My dad believed in taking flyers, and he took his share. He tested new ideas in business, experimented with new strategies, and tried new products. He took a certain number of risks with people and with investments.

Some flyers worked out well for him and paid off handsomely. Others crashed and he paid dearly. But when a crash occurred, he would tell me about the lessons he'd learned and about the joy he'd had during the adventure. "It's only money," he'd say. "It's not the end of the world."

It didn't faze him a bit if people rolled their eyes at one of his long shots. He seemed almost impervious to nay-sayers. When people told him he was nuts for considering some new venture or flyer, he would just smile broadly and reply from some secure interior place, "You're probably right. We're all going to find out in a few months, aren't we?" But he never let the approval ratings of his peers affect his risk-assessment capability. He was neither a careless risk-taker, nor was he risk-averse. He just believed that a calculated flyer here and there would keep him on the cutting edge of growth.

A few years ago, Willow decided to take a calculated risk and start a Gen-X ministry called Axis. We didn't know much about this, but we hired a few staff members, said some prayers, and took off. Presently there are nearly 2,000 eighteen- to twenty-eight-year-olds attending our Axis services. It is one of the most exciting ministries in our church. I'm really glad we took that flyer.

As I mentioned in an earlier chapter, we recently took another flyer when we decided to try to raise 70 million dollars—50 million in cash along with the 20 million we had already put aside—to address future building needs. Yes, there was considerable risk involved. But God blessed our efforts tremendously. I'm glad we took that flyer.

Currently we're taking another flyer with our new Regional Ministry Centers. We don't know how well these centers are going to work; they might fail. But because we believe they are Spirit-led calculated risks, we are choosing to invest both people and resources into them.

Here's the point: Some leaders are extravagant risk-takers who are killing their churches. They're risking way too much way too often. The problem may be that there's a bet-the-farm risk-taker informing their decision-making process, convincing them that the higher the risk the better.

In contrast, other leaders are almost totally risk-averse. They haven't taken a flyer in their adult life. They probably have someone behind the scenes whose influence whispers, "Risk is bad. If you fail, it will be the end of the world."

Who is informing your risk assessment? Do you know? Is it time to review your list of mentors? Might it be time to appoint some new advisors who could raise or lower your risk profile according to your need?

CONSULTING MENTORS ABOUT PERFORMANCE EVALUATIONS

ONE OF THE MOST complex issues I face at Willow is how to handle under-performing staff. The minute I realize I'm going to have to make a decision related to this, I go on high alert. Why? Because this involves people, and as previously mentioned, one of my core beliefs is that people are God's greatest treasures. Consequently, I never consider these matters lightly. Often during conversations about staff performance I am silently pondering the teachings of the two men who have most shaped my thinking on this issue. Who are they? Jesus and Peter Drucker—in that order, of course.

Echoing in my mind during such discussions is Jesus' statement, "A laborer is worthy of his hire" (Luke 10:7). The implication is that an employer who is receiving effective, valuable, consistent service from an employee should afford appropriate wages and honor to that employee. This same teaching, however, implies that if an employer is *not* receiving effective, valuable, consistent service from a worker, then the worker is no longer worthy of his or her full hire. The wages should cease, or at least decrease.

Peter Drucker once told me, "Bill, when it comes to paid staff, even church staff, under-performance is unacceptable." I've never forgotten that. So when it's brought to my attention that we have an under-performing staff member, we react quickly. We call it what it is: unacceptable.

But then we immediately try to discern the cause of the under-performance. Is it a poor job fit or inadequate training? Do we have unrealistic goals or expectations for this person? Is he or she being poorly managed? If so, the church is at fault and should be held accountable. It is horribly unfair to blame employees for poor performance when they are not receiving the coaching, mentoring, training, or managing that they need. In fact, if there are a number of employees performing poorly it may be prudent to examine the performance of their supervisor to see if it's a leadership problem rather than an employee performance problem.

If an employee's poor performance, however, stems from unhealthy relating patterns, issues with authority, dishonesty, or old-fashioned laziness, we must bring that to the employee's attention forthrightly, and put a plan for improvement into place immediately.

Hopefully we can turn things around. But if after many months of diligent effort on both sides, the staff person remains unable to deliver effective, valuable, consistent service to the church, even tougher conversations will follow. If those conversations don't lead to resolution, employment will most likely be terminated.

Whenever we are forced to let staff members go, we offer gracious severance packages and whatever transitional support might be appropriate. But extending grace does not mean closing our eyes to the truth in order to "be nice" or to avoid uncomfortable conversations or tough decisions. Grace does not mean that we should carry a staff person who isn't performing adequately. "A laborer is worthy of his hire," but if we're not receiving the proper labor, the deal is off. Under-performance is unacceptable.

I was once addressing staffing issues in a mentoring group. At one point an older pastor from a mainline denomination started shaking his head and said, "You're making it sound like you could actually fire a staff member who was making trouble."

"Well," I responded. "I don't know if I want to put it that tersely, but yes, eventually we could, and would."

He said, "I could never do that."

"Why not?" I asked.

"Because my denomination makes it almost impossible to remove a staff member. In fact, I probably couldn't fire my associate pastor if he was having sex with the organist on top of the organ during the 10:00 A.M. service!"

"Well . . . ," I replied, "That is a problem—and I am glad it's yours and not mine!" I went on to suggest that the whole denomination should reexamine their personnel policies.

In my opinion, many churches and church leaders need to do that. The place to start is by reflecting on who informs your decision-making regarding hiring and managing paid staff. Do you know? Are they the right informers? Is it time for a change?

CONSULTING MY EXCELLENCE MENTORS

SCRIPTURE HAS MUCH TO say regarding the value of excellence, so we have claimed it as one of the big-ten values of our church. We say it this way, "Excellence honors God and inspires people."

When I have to make a decision pertaining to the value of excellence, I think of two businessmen from Michigan. One is Ed Prince. Before he died several years ago, he was the driving force behind the Prince Corporation, a leading manufacturer of automotive components. The other is Rich DeVos, co-founder of the Amway Corporation.

The levels of excellence that these two Dutch, Christian Reformed entrepreneurs established in their businesses and personal lives have always inspired me. Often, when I have to make a decision regarding a level of excellence, I think, *Oh man, I wish Ed were still here.* Or, *I wish I could call Rich right now and get his opinion.* Then I reflect on the choices I have seen these men make in similar situations throughout the years. The actions they took in the past help inform my decisions today. Who does that for you? Do you have an excellence guru?

CONSULTING MY MORALE INFORMER

MY FRIEND JOHN MAXWELL, to whom I referred in the last chapter, often comes to mind when I am trying to improve staff morale at Willow. Whenever I see staff shoulders slumping I simply ask myself the question, "What would John do right now?" Then I call to mind what I've seen him do hundreds of times in other settings where people are battling discouragement. He puts his arm around them and thanks them for being on the team. He listens patiently as they describe their heartaches. Then he offers a sincere thirty-second prayer of encouragement. By the time he walks away, their spirits truly have been lifted.

In case you haven't realized this yet, morale is a big deal. In my opinion, thousands of congregations all around the world are suffering from "motivation malnourishment." At training conferences I sometimes ask church volunteers when they last received a note of encouragement from their pastor or staff supervisor. Most often they say something like this: "I never have. I've been serving for twenty years and I've never received a personal commendation from anyone on our leadership team. I'm sure they appreciate what I do, but no one has ever actually told me that."

We leaders must do better. Our devoted workers deserve a regularly administered "atta boy" or "atta girl."

We've improved in this regard at Willow in recent years. We try to offer personal thanks throughout the year, but in addition we pull out all the stops to say a public "Thank You" with our Annual Volunteer Celebration Event. As I mentioned in an earlier chapter, this has become a really big deal. Every year we try to do something a little different to honor our unpaid staff.

Recently we took a creative flyer at our Celebration Event. During our midweek New Community service, we lined up hundreds of our volunteers and mimicked a small-town parade. John Ortberg and Nancy Beach played the Regis and Kathy Lee roles. They emceed the event, describing each different ministry group as it paraded across the stage. The volunteers were waving signs, the congregation was cheering, music was blaring, and photographs of volunteers at work were flashing on the screens.

Afterwards I admitted to one of the participants that the parade idea was a little loony. To my surprise, this person said, "I've been a volunteer here for eighteen years. I love it and I'd do it whether anyone noticed or not. But I have to confess, having the whole church cheer for me and for my fellow volunteers was like … well, let me just say you can come up with as many of those loony ideas as you want. It will be okay by me!"

Morale is a big deal. When morale is sagging, it's the leader's job to spot it and lift it up. Who comes to your mind as a role model for this? Who do you know who encourages the spirit and lifts the hearts of staff and volunteers? Let them inform your decisions about issues related to morale. Your staff, paid and unpaid, will be glad you did.

I could talk about many other leaders who inform my decision-making. For theological decisions, I have Dr. Bilezikian. I have several other advisors who help me in the areas of finance, psychology, and relationships. I would be lost without the wisdom these people offer me.

What if you don't have mentors in some of these areas? My recommendation would be to read often and widely and to try to spend time with other leaders as often as possible. This will expose you to people and principles that can gradually inform your daily decisions. Over time God will help you identify the inner core of consultants who can best help you to make God-honoring decisions.

MY THIRD DATA SOURCE: PAIN

OFTEN STAFF MEMBERS COME to my office to promote ministry plans they want me to support. Sometimes, to their great surprise, I cut them off mid-sentence. "I've heard enough," I say. "Count me out." Thinking I'm kidding, they continue trying to convince me. So I jump in again, "No. Not in my lifetime. It's just not going to happen."

By then they realize I'm serious. If they ask, "Why?" I might say something like this: "We tried that very same thing fifteen years ago. We thought we were smart, but we got whacked. We tried it again ten years ago and we got whacked again. Three years ago we took another pass at it, and we really got whacked. So we have far exceeded our whack tolerance. I understand why your proposal sounds good to you; it sounded good to us too. But it isn't good. So I mean it when I say this idea is DOA—dead on arrival. It's not going to happen, so just let it go."

One of the advantages of experience is that it provides veteran leaders with a "pain file" of raw-edged memories. The lessons gathered in this file help leaders to discern the level of potential pain inherent in any new idea. If the level is too high, their danger sirens start blaring, and they know they have to pull the plug. Younger, lesser-experienced leaders are still taking unwise flyers and collecting their whacks.

Several years ago at the WCA's annual Leadership Summit, when I first introduced the "three Cs"—character, competence, and chemistry—as the basis for staff hiring, I said, "Never compromise on character. And when it comes to competence, shoot high; go after the best people you can. Concerning chemistry, make sure the person fits in well with existing team members." I ended that lecture by saying, "I've taken enough beatings. I've seen and caused enough bloodshed. I'm never going to knowingly violate the three Cs again."

After that summit several pastors wrote and challenged me about those three Cs. When I got their letters I just smiled and filed them. I'm not trying to be cocky, but I knew what was going to happen. Sure enough, some months later I received a second letter from one of those pastors. Sheepishly he admitted that maybe character was more important than he had initially thought. He went on to describe the staff horror story that had recently unfolded at his church, ending his letter with these words, "I will never again compromise character in the selection of a leader."

Another pastor wrote, "I hated the idea of qualifying or disqualifying somebody on the basis of how well they related to existing team members—that chemistry thing. So despite an obvious 'edge' to his personality, I added a highly competent local contractor to our building committee. Within months he had managed to polarize everybody on the committee and to change all the dynamics on the team. Now I have a royal mess on my hands. I've got great volunteers bailing out, and the building is only half up."

My words back to these pastors were to this effect, "I feel your pain. I've had plenty of my own. There's just one thing to do at times like this: Learn from your mistakes."

Pain is a powerful teacher and a fantastic informer of our decision-making process.

I take an unwritten pain file with me wherever I go. If for some reason I am tempted to make another payment to the pain piper, I ask myself if I really want to get banged over the head again. *Do I really need to add more pain to my life?*

Have you ever taken the time to develop a "Top Ten Pain List"? Sometimes in mentoring sessions with pastors, we sit around after dinner and tell each other about the lessons we've learned the hard way. In sometimes humorous detail we describe the stuff we'll never do again. I've heard some doozies.

One guy said, "I'll never make my mother-in-law the head elder again." Another pastor said, "I'll never let a guest speaker teach on signs and wonders while I'm on vacation." A particularly easy-going pastor said, "I'll never again tell the worship dancer, 'Just wear whatever you want when you dance at the morning service.' Big mistake!"

These are all true stories. Pain-filled stories. But potentially, very valuable sources of data.

We leaders need to keep files of such stories and review them often so that we don't inflict unnecessary pain on ourselves or on our churches by repeating mistakes of the past. Pain can be a very effective teacher, but only if we pay attention and learn the hard lessons.

One last word about pain. Proverbs 13:20 says, "Whoever walks with wise people will be wise." In other words, if we are wise we will learn from the experiences of others, including their pain. This is another reason why it's so important to get together with other leaders and ask, "What's working for you? What's not? Where did you get whacked? How badly?" The reason I have never tried to hide my ministry mistakes is that I hope other leaders will learn from my frequent foul-ups and spare their people the pain I have caused Willow.

ONE FINAL DATA SOURCE: THE HOLY SPIRIT

THE HOLY SPIRIT IS, by far, the most valuable data source we have. Leadership training and mentoring are good. Honing our skills is admirable. Seeking wise counsel is beneficial. Developing our minds is essential. But ultimately we walk by faith, not by sight. There is a supernatural dimension to leadership that only comes our way when we listen carefully to the Spirit.

One December the programming team was twisting my arm to decide the topic of our upcoming January weekend series. So when my schedule allowed, I went away for a day of solitude so I could think and pray and ask for God's guidance. As definitely as I've ever received a prompting for a weekend series, I sensed the Holy Spirit whisper, "Bill, this January preach on love." Being the huge man of faith that I am, I replied in my spirit, "You've got to be kidding. Love is too squishy for January. People need their annual January body slam. Stuff like: fly straight this year; lose weight; slow down; get out of debt; stop sinning; grow in God. There are plenty of themes that 'preach well' in January—but love's not one of them."

But the Holy Spirit eventually wore me down, and I raised the white flag of surrender. Several weeks later I launched a series called "Graduate Level Loving." From the moment I opened my mouth for the first installment of that series it was obvious that God's spirit was working overtime. "Whoa," I thought. "Something major is going on here."

It was one of the most highly responded-to series in recent years and has since been used by churches all over the world. Every time I hear of another church benefiting from that series, I am humbled and reminded that those messages were driven not by pastoral common sense but by a clear prompting from God. And as I look back over almost thirty years of Christian leadership, I can easily recall scores of decisions that made me look smart but had almost nothing to do with my insight or with the clever machinations of my mind. Instead, those decisions had everything to do with the gracious guidance of the Holy Spirit.

Want a few examples? The decision to start Willow leaps to mind. Most people assume Willow was the fulfillment of a personal ambition or a carefully calculated marketing plan. In reality, it grew from a very definite prompting from God to start a church to reach out to the parents of the kids attending our youth ministry. The same could be said about Willow's focus on reaching seekers. That has always been a Spirit-prompted choice. The same is true of our decision to utilize the arts and our decision to do our believers' service at midweek. All those decisions defied conventional wisdom at the time. They were strictly the result of following the Spirit's promptings.

Surely we must use wisdom and good judgment as we lead our churches. But just as surely, we must at all times turn an ear to heaven. We must listen as the Holy Spirit, our supernatural data source, speaks into our decision-making process the wisdom we need the most.

I used to assume that all Christian leaders turned to the Holy Spirit as the data source that superceded all others. But over the years I've learned otherwise. So let me end this chapter by posing a few questions that may help us focus attention on our ultimate data source.

Is there enough quietness in your life for you to hear the whispers of the Holy Spirit? Do you have the guts to carry out promptings, even though you might not understand them fully, and even though your team might question your wisdom? Are you willing to walk by faith? Will you commit yourself to allowing the Spirit to fully inform your decision-making?

When a leader combines the promptings of the Holy Spirit with the other sources of decision-making data—core convictions, influencing mentors, and the lessons of pain—that leader will operate with ever-increasing levels of decision-making prowess.

If you didn't know better, you might even think that leader had a sixth sense!

CHAPTER NINE

The Art of Self-leadership

The 360-Degree Leader

IMAGINE A COMPASS WITH A SILVER CASE, A ROUND WHITE FACE, A slender black needle, and four letters placed at ninety-degree intervals—N, S, E, and W. Almost every time the word *leadership* is mentioned, in what direction do leaders instinctively think?

South.

Say the word *leadership* and most leaders' minds migrate to the people who are under their care. When they go to leadership conferences they assume they have only one goal: to improve their ability to lead the people God has entrusted to them.

South. It's a leader's first instinct.

What many people don't realize is that to lead well, a leader actually needs to be able to lead in all directions—north, south, east, and west.

For example, effective leaders have to lead north, which means leading those who are over them. Through relationship and influence good leaders lead the people who supervise them. Much of what I do at Willow Creek, through relationship, prayer, and casting vision, is to try to gently influence those who have authority over me, the board of directors and the elders.

Effective leaders must also learn how to lead east and west, in peer-group settings. If we don't learn how to lead laterally and create win-win situations with colleagues, an entire church culture can deteriorate.

So a leader must learn how to lead down, up, and laterally. But perhaps the most overlooked leadership challenge is the one in the middle.

WHO IS YOUR TOUGHEST LEADERSHIP CHALLENGE?

You.

Consider 1 Samuel 30. David, the future king of Israel, is a young leader just learning to lead his troops into battle. Though David's a novice, God is pouring his favor on him so most of the battles are going his way. Then on one seemingly normal day that pattern changes. After returning home from fighting on one front, David and his men discover that enemy soldiers have come around their flanks and attacked and destroyed their campsite, dragging off the women and children and burning all their belongings.

This would define a bad day for any leader, but it's not over yet. David's soldiers are tired, angry, and worried sick about their families. They're miffed at God. Finally a faction of them spreads word that they have had it with David's leadership. They figure that the entire tragedy is David's fault, and they decide to stone him to death.

Suddenly David is facing a severe leadership crisis. Immediately he has to decide where to direct his leadership energy. Who needs it most? His soldiers? The officers? The faction of rebels?

His answer? None of the above.

In this critical moment David realizes a fundamental truth: he needs to lead *himself* before he can lead anybody else. Unless he is squared away internally he has nothing much to offer his team. So he found a place of solitude, and there "David strengthened himself in the Lord his God" (1 Samuel 30:6). Only then does he attempt to fire up his team to rescue their families and what's left of their belongings.

David understood the importance of self-leadership. Although this issue is rarely discussed, make no mistake, it is an essential part of leadership. How can any of us lead others effectively if our spirits are sagging or our courage is wavering?

Not long ago I read an article that seriously messed with my mind. Acclaimed leadership expert Dee Hock challenged leaders to calculate how much time and energy they invest in each of these directions: leading people under their care (S), leading people over them (N), leading people laterally (E–W), and leading themselves. Since he's been thinking and writing about leadership for over twenty years and is a laureate in the Business Hall of Fame, I was eager to gain from his wisdom.

His recommendation? "It is management of self that should occupy 50 percent of our time and the best of our ability. And when we do that the ethical, moral, and spiritual elements of management are inescapable."[1] I was stunned. Did he really mean this? That we should devote 50 percent of our time to self-leadership, and divide the remaining 50 percent between leading up, leading down, and leading laterally? His suggested percentages bothered me so much I couldn't finish the article. I tucked it away in my desk drawer to give his ideas a few hours to simmer in my mind.

While they simmered I read an article by Daniel Goleman, the author of the best-selling book *Emotional Intelligence*. Since the release of that book, Goleman has spent much of his time analyzing why a small percentage of leaders develop to their fullest potential while most leaders hit a plateau far beneath what one might expect from them.

---

[1]From "The Art of Chaordic Leadership," *Leader to Leader* (Winter 2000), 22.

His conclusion? The difference has to do with (you guessed it) self-leadership. He calls it "emotional self-control." According to Goleman, this form of self-control is exhibited by leaders when they persevere in leadership despite overwhelming opposition or discouragement; when they refuse to give up during times of crisis; when they manage to hold ego at bay; and when they stay focused on their mission rather than being distracted by other peoples' agendas.

Goleman contends that exceptional leaders distinguish themselves because they "know their strengths, their limits, and their weaknesses."[2] As I read Goleman's corroborating data, I thought, *Maybe Dee Hock's percentages aren't all that absurd!*

Recall the first five chapters of Mark's Gospel. Do you remember Jesus' pattern of intense ministry activity quickly followed by time set aside for reflection, prayer, fasting, and solitude? Jesus repeated that pattern throughout his ministry. In our terms, Jesus was practicing the art of self-leadership. He knew he needed to go to a quiet place and recalibrate. He knew he needed to remind himself who he was and how much the Father loved him. Even Jesus needed to invest regularly in keeping his calling clear, avoiding mission drift, and keeping distraction, discouragement, and temptation at bay.

This is self-leadership. And nobody—I mean nobody—can do this work for us. Every leader has to do this work alone, and it isn't easy. In fact, Dee Hock claims that because it's such tough work most leaders avoid it. We would rather try to inspire or control the behavior of others than face the rigorous work of self-reflection and inner growth.

Some years ago a top Christian leader disqualified himself from ministry. A published article described his demise: "[He] sank like a

---

[2]From "The Emotional Intelligence of Leaders," *Leader to Leader* (Fall 1998), 22.

rock, beat up, burned out, angry and depressed, no good to himself and no good to the people he loved." When this pastor finally wrote publicly about his experience, he said, "Eventually I couldn't even sleep at night. Another wave of broken lives would come to shore at the church, and I found I didn't have enough compassion for them any more. And inside I became angry, angry, angry. Many people still wonder whatever happened to me. They think I had a crisis of faith. The fact is I simply collapsed on the inside."

Dee Hock would probably suggest that he had failed the self-leadership test. Before his crash, he should have called a timeout to regroup, reflect, and recalibrate. He should have taken a sabbatical or sought Christian counseling. Daniel Goleman would say this guy lost his emotional self-control. And he ended up paying a high price.

I'll never forget the day three wise advisors came to me on behalf of the church. They said, "Bill, there were two eras during the first twenty years of Willow Creek's history when, by your own admission, you were not at your leadership best: once in the late seventies and again in the early nineties. The data shows that Willow Creek paid dearly for your leadership fumble. It cost all of us more than you'll ever know."

Then they said words I'll never forget: "The best gift you can give the people you lead here at Willow is a healthy, energized, fully surrendered, and focused self. And no one can make that happen in your life except you. It's up to you to make the right choices so you can be at your best." While they were talking, the Holy Spirit was saying, "They're right, Bill. They're right."

Because I know what's at stake, I now ask myself several self-leadership questions on a regular basis.

IS MY CALLING SURE?

ON THIS MATTER, I'm from the old school. I really believe that anyone who bears the name of Jesus Christ has a calling, whether they're a pastor or a layperson. We all must surrender ourselves fully and make ourselves completely available to God. We must all ask, "What's my mission, God? Where do you want me to serve? What role would you have me play in your grand kingdom drama?"

Remember what Paul said about his calling? "I consider my life worth nothing to me, if only I may finish the race and complete the task the Lord Jesus has given me" (Acts 20:24). For Paul, there was no higher priority than fulfilling the ministry God had given him.

It is a great privilege and blessing to receive a call from the holy God. Our life becomes focused. We have increased energy and greater confidence. And knowing that we're on a mission that matters adds purpose and meaning to every day. But we can only enjoy these benefits if we keep our calling sure.

In recent years I have come to understand that it is my job to do just that. So on a regular basis I ask, *God, are you still calling me to be the pastor of Willow Creek and to help churches around the world?* When I receive divine reaffirmation of that calling, I say, "Then let's go. Let's ignore all other distractions and temptations. Let's burn the bridges and get on with it!"

If you've been called to be a leader it's your responsibility to keep your calling sure. With an open heart, seek God's affirmation. If you don't receive it, then pull out the stops to discern what God is trying to tell you. If you do get God's continued affirmation of your calling, then do whatever you have to do to stay focused on it. Post it on your refrigerator. Frame it and put it on your desk. Keep it foremost in your mind.

IS MY VISION CLEAR?

HOW CAN I LEAD people into the future if my picture of the future is fuzzy? Every year we have a Vision Night at Willow Creek. You know who started Vision Night? I did. You know whom I do it for primarily? Me. You know why? Because Vision Night forces me to be crystal clear about my vision for Willow.

I believe that every leader needs a regularly scheduled Vision Night. On that night we say, "This is the picture of the future we believe God has given us; this is what we're going to do; this is why we're going to do it; and this is how we're going to do it. And if we all pray like crazy and link arms together and stay focused on our mission, we will be a different and better church one year from now."

At Willow we prepare very diligently for Vision Night. Weeks in advance our senior leaders hold meetings to discuss future plans. We write the main ideas on flip charts and laptops, then refine them and distribute them in draft form. We each spend hours praying over these drafts and in searching the Scriptures. Finally we ask, "God, is this what you would have?" By the time Vision Night rolls around the vision is crystal clear again. I am the primary person insisting that we go through this process every year because as the senior pastor I need to be absolutely clear about the vision.

IS MY PASSION HOT?

HAVE YOU EVER WONDERED whose responsibility it is to keep a leader's passion fired up? You guessed it. That's a self-leadership fundamental.

Last year at an elders' meeting, one of the elders asked me, "As busy as you are, why do you fly out on Friday nights to speak in some small, out-of-the-way church to help raise money or dedicate a new facility? Why do you do that?"

My answer: Because it keeps my passion hot.

I explained that earlier in the year I had helped a church in California dedicate their new building. As I entered their new auditorium, one guy took me to the corner of their spacious venue and peeled the carpet back to show me the area of concrete where everyone in the core of the church had inscribed the names of their family and friends who are far from God. When the wet cement dried they covered it over with carpet. Now every month the core believers stand over the inscribed names of their loved ones and pray fervently for their salvation. I explained to the elders that I was buzzed during the entire flight back to Chicago.

That church fired me up. It inspired me. I preached better the following Saturday and Sunday for having made that Friday night visit. I have come to understand that my passion has to be white hot before I can expect Willow to catch it. So I have to keep it hot. If helping struggling churches on Friday nights helps me stay fired up—then I better clear my calendar and make that a priority.

We do hundreds of conferences through the Willow Creek Association. Sometimes senior pastors of flourishing churches pull me aside and whisper, "I have to come here once or twice a year just to keep my fires lit." They seem embarrassed about coming to Willow so often, as if it's a sign of weakness.

I tell them, "You're a leader. It's your job to keep your passion hot. Do whatever you have to do, read whatever you have to read, go wherever you have to go to stay fired up. And don't apologize to anybody."

AM I DEVELOPING MY GIFTS?

POP QUIZ: WHAT ARE your top three spiritual gifts? If you can't articulate them as quickly as you can give your name, address, and phone number, I'm tempted to say, "You need your cage rattled!" Before you write me a note telling me I've made you feel bad, I need to let you know that when it comes to this issue, I have a Sympathy Deficit Disorder. Maybe I need medication or time on a shrink's couch, but I have very little sympathy for leaders who are fuzzy about their spiritual gifts. Leaders must know which gifts they've been given and in what order.

The Bible teaches that all leaders are accountable before God for developing each of their gifts to the zenith of their potential.

God has entrusted me with three gifts. Some people have been given five, six, or seven. I have only three—leadership, evangelism, and teaching—but I know that I have been called by God to develop and stretch them to the best of my ability. That's why I read everything I can that pertains to these gifts and why I hang around as often as possible with people who are better than I am in these areas.

I never forget that someday I'm going to stand before God and be held accountable for how I developed what he entrusted to me. When that time comes I really do want to receive a commendation from him for faithfulness in each of my areas of giftedness.

Fellow leaders, are you challenging yourself to develop your gifts to the best of your ability? Self-leadership demands that we do.

IS MY CHARACTER SUBMITTED TO CHRIST?

LEADERSHIP ALSO REQUIRES MORAL authority. Followers will only trust leaders who exhibit the highest levels of integrity. People will not follow a leader with moral incongruities for long. Every time you compromise character you compromise leadership.

Some time ago one of our staff members was frustrated in his leadership role because certain people under his supervision seemed to be uncooperative. I started poking around his department to figure out what was wrong. Then the real picture emerged. One person said, "He sets meetings and then he doesn't show up." Another said, "He rarely returns phone calls." Someone else said, "Often we don't know where he is."

I scheduled a meeting with that leader and verified the assessments of his teammates. Then I looked him square in the eyes and said, "Let's get something straight. When you tell your teammates that you'll be at a certain place at a certain time and you are late or don't show up, that's a character issue. When you promise to return a phone call and then neglect to do so, that makes people feel devalued. When your teammates don't know where you are during work hours, that erodes trust. You need to clean this stuff up or we'll have to move you out." Over the years I have seen that if character issues are compromised, it hurts the whole team and eventually undermines the mission.

Who wants to be a leader who demoralizes the troops and hurts the cause? I certainly don't. So on a regular basis I sing Rory Noland's song during my times alone with God:

> Holy Spirit, take control.
> Take my body, mind, and soul.
> Put a finger on anything that doesn't please you,
> Anything I do that grieves you.
> Holy Spirit, take control.[3]

Whose job is it to maintain a leader's character? It's the leader's job, of course.

IS MY PRIDE SUBDUED?

FIRST PETER 5:5 SAYS, "God opposes the proud but he gives grace to the humble." Do you know what Peter is saying? That as leaders we have a choice. Do we want opposition from God as we lead or do we want his grace and favor?

If you're a sailor, you know how difficult it is to sail upwind. You also know how wonderful and relaxing it is to sail downwind. Peter is saying, "Which way do you want it? Do you want to sail upwind or downwind? If you clothe yourself in humility, the favor of God will carry you. If you're proud, you'll be sailing into the wind."

Do you want to know the best way to find out if pride is affecting your leadership?

Ask.

Ask your teammates. Ask the people in your small group. Ask your spouse. Ask your elders or board members. Ask your friends,

---

[3]Rory Noland, "Holy Spirit Take Control," Ever Devoted Music, 1984.

"Do you ever sense a prideful spirit in my leadership? Do the words I speak ever convey a spirit of arrogance?" If you can't even ask a question like that, then you probably do have a pride issue. This is no problem if you like sailing into a stiff wind. But how much better to have a humble spirit and be carried by God.

If you have a pride problem don't ignore it. Pray for the Holy Spirit's help. Talk to wise mentors. Visit a counselor. Do whatever you have to do to subdue your pride. It's your job.

AM I OVERCOMING FEAR?

FEAR CAN BE IMMOBILIZING. Sometimes I ask pastors who are grieved because their churches are dying, "Why haven't you introduced change?" I ask business leaders who are hesitating to launch a new product, "Why haven't you taken the step?" I ask political leaders who are waffling on issues they claim to feel strongly about, "Why haven't you taken a public stand?" Often the response is: "Because I am afraid." Fear immobilizes and neutralizes leaders.

Believe me I am not above letting fear mess with my decision-making. I remember the morning in the year 2000 when it became clear to me that we needed to launch a $70 million building program. Our vision for the future was clear. The elders, the board of directors, and the management team had all signed off on it. The last step in the equation was for me to have the guts to launch the public phase of the effort. But you know what swirled around in my mind? *The minute you go public with a 70-million-dollar campaign, there's no backing out. It's pass-fail.* I realized that everything we had worked for over the past twenty-five years was on the line. All the credibility our congregation has established in our community and around the world was at stake. The fear kept building. *What if we fall $20 million short? Why expose Willow to that kind of disappointment? We're cruising along. We're growing and baptizing a thousand people a year. A huge misstep could blow everything up. Why take this risk?*

But at a certain point I realized what I was doing: letting fear sabotage my leadership. I reminded myself of that little verse 1 John 4:4, "The one who is in you is greater than the one who is in the world." I asked myself: *Has God spoken to me? Has he made his direction clear? Is he still going to love me if I fail? Am I still going to heaven if this whole thing doesn't turn out right?* I struggled, but finally I found the courage to step out in faith.

It's a leader's job to deal with fear so it doesn't sabotage our mission.

ARE INTERIOR ISSUES UNDERMINING MY LEADERSHIP?

ALL OF US HAVE experienced wounds, losses, and disappointments in our past. That brokenness has helped shape—or misshape—us into who we are today. I laugh at people who say, "My family of origin issues have not affected me." Or, "Nothing in my past impacts my life today."

Leaders who ignore their interior reality often make unwise decisions that have grave consequences for the people they lead. Often they're completely unaware of what's driving such decisions. Some pastors don't realize that their own struggles with grandiosity cause them to make decisions that enslave their entire congregation to an agenda that's not God's. It's an agenda that comes straight out of their need to be bigger than, better than, grander than.

Other leaders are incurable people pleasers. Every week they take a poll to see where they stand in the ratings, then behave accordingly.

Who is responsible for processing and resolving our interior issues so our churches won't be negatively impacted by our junk? You are. I am.

I've spent plenty of time in a Christian counselor's office. I am still in contact with two Christian counselors. To this day I keep a list of questions regarding aspects of myself that are confusing.

Questions like: Why did I say that? Why did I power up over that person? Why did I acquiesce in that situation when firmness was required? It's my responsibility to sort these things out with a friend, a spiritual director, or a Christian counselor. Self-leadership demands that I do.

IS MY PACE SUSTAINABLE?

As I've previously mentioned, I came close to a total emotional meltdown in the early 1990s. Suffice it to say I was not practicing self-leadership. I didn't understand the principle of sustainability. So I fried my emotions. I abused my spiritual gifts. I damaged my body. I neglected my family and friends. And I came within a whisker of becoming a ministry statistic.

I remember sitting in a restaurant and writing: "The pace at which I've been doing the work of God is destroying God's work in me." Then, still sitting in that restaurant, I put my head down on my spiral notebook and sobbed.

After mopping up, I said, *God, what's going on here?* I sensed the Holy Spirit saying, *Bill, who has a gun to your head? Who is forcing you to bite off more than you can chew? Who is intimidating you into overcommitting? Whose approval and affirmation and applause other than God's are you seeking? What makes you live this way?* The answers were worse than sobering. They were devastating.

The elders, to whom I'm accountable, were not the cause of my pace problem. Nor were the board of directors, the staff, my family, or my friends. My whole pace problem was of my own making.

I sat all alone in that cheap restaurant in South Haven, Michigan, foot-stomping mad that I couldn't point the finger at anybody else for my exhaustion and my emotional numbness. It's a terribly lonely feeling to have no one to blame. It's rotten to realize that to find the bad guy, you just have to look in a mirror.

The truth that we all have to accept is that the only person who can put a sustainability program together for us is *us*. Month after month for fifteen years I was overscheduled and my life was out of control. Deep down I kept wondering, *Why aren't the elders rescuing me? Why aren't my friends rescuing me? Don't people see I'm dying?*

Finally the voice of self-leadership whispered the truth in my ear: *It is your responsibility to devise a sustainability plan and stick to it every day.* By God's grace I eventually sorted out how to do that and now, twelve years later, I can honestly say that my pace in life and ministry is sustainable and I am more joyful than at any other time in my life.

I am grateful for my more realistic pace not only for my sake but for my wife's sake as well. We leaders are naïve if we think we can live at an unhealthy pace without causing pain to those closest to us. Because Lynne is wholeheartedly committed to the ministry of the local church, she has always done her best to support my work at Willow as well as my travels domestically and internationally. The imbalance in my life, however, made supporting me a much bigger task for her than it should have been. She ended up handling far too many home and family responsibilities alone, greatly limiting the time and energy she had for developing her own gifts and ministry.

I conscientiously committed my time to my children, knowing I couldn't expect them to accept an absent dad, but like too many pastors, I expected my wife to understand and accept my extreme commitment to "God's work." That was a mistake, a self-leadership fumble. Our marriage suffered, as does any marriage caught up in the pressure of an insane pace.

By God's grace, that era is well behind us. We rejoice in the close bonds we have with our young adult children and in the true renewal of our relationship. For us, the "good old days" are today and the future looks bright.

But we would not be in this place had I not come to grips with my schedule. Leaders, please listen. You've got to let go of the illusion that there's someone "out there" who ought to be rescuing you. Establishing a sustainable pace for your life is nobody's job but yours. So do it. Your life, your ministry, your marriage, your family—they all depend on it.

IS MY LOVE FOR GOD AND PEOPLE INCREASING?

HAVE YOU REMINDED YOURSELF recently whose job it is to fuel the flames of your love? Is it the church's job? Your spouse's job? Your small group's job? No. It's *your* job and *my* job to make sure our love for God and for other people is increasing. Nobody can do that for us.

Chapter 11 is devoted to the subject of deepening our love relationship with God, so in the concluding pages of this chapter I'd like to focus on the second part of the love challenge: loving others.

If it's true, as I claimed in Chapter 8, that people are God's greatest treasure, then it follows that they ought to be our greatest treasure too. If they're our greatest treasure, then our hearts ought to be overflowing with love for them. Church work ought to be, at its core, the work of loving people like God loves them.

Yet I reached a point in my life where I realized that my heart for people was not growing, but shrinking. I was loving people not more, but less.

Strange as it may sound, I can often measure the size of my heart by what happens the first days of my annual summer study break. For many years, when I finished an intense ministry season at Willow and drove over to the little town where my family and I spend our summers I honestly didn't give a rip about the people in that town. My attitude was, "Hey, I gave back at the Chicago office. You are not my problem." Sad to say, my heart was pretty small in those days.

I tried to justify my indifference, but I knew it wasn't right. So I decided to make several life-management adjustments during my ministry year in an attempt to keep my heart from shrinking and my spirit from getting callused. I began taking regular days off, scheduled more solitude into my week, and incorporated into my reading diet more books that were challenging on a deeply spiritual level.

Several years ago, a few days into my break, a young man who had heard I was a pastor tracked me down at the marina where I keep my boat. He was twenty-five years old, fresh out of jail with a list of problems as long as your arm. After telling me his woes, he boldly asked me for guidance, money, and anything else I had to give.

I really did sense that he was earnestly hoping to make some changes in his life so I listened patiently, then said, "Let me sleep on this and I'll get back to you." Later that night I tried to explain to Lynne what I was feeling. "All the odds are stacked against this guy," I said. "For the rest of his life he's probably going to struggle because of his past mistakes. And maybe he's just going to keep on making them. But maybe if somebody gave him a little help, he could make some positive progress. Let's try to do something for him."

I wasn't surprised that Lynne supported my idea. What surprised me is that *I* supported my idea. I'm sorry to have to confess how shocked I was by the compassion that welled up in my heart for this guy. That's how long it had been since I'd ended a long ministry season with enough energy to truly care about the plight of another human being.

So we gave him a little money to carry him through the current crisis, then helped him find some odd jobs that provided him with a somewhat steady income. During the summer I met with him quite often and we became friends. Interacting with him that summer represented a kind of self-leadership victory for me. Over and over the Holy Spirit whispered to me, "You're growing, Bill. Your heart is getting bigger. Way to go!"

I never want to let my heart shrivel again. I am more determined now than ever to make sure my heart keeps growing bigger during the remainder of my leadership adventure. What good does it do to be a Christian leader if my skills, my insights, my decisions, and my energy don't flow from a deep love for God and for other people?

How's your heart? If you stay on the track you are on, will your heart grow bigger as the ministry years go by? Or are your margins too thin? Are you running so fast that by the time you reach periodic finish lines you're a depleted wreck? Please face what you need to face. Change what you have to change. Experiment with life-management practices that will allow you to excel at leadership *and* excel at loving.

North, south, east, and west—a leader must learn to lead in all these directions. But it doesn't matter how many points you manage to hit around the compass if you aren't strong in the middle. If reading this chapter made you squirm, then read it again. Ask yourself the questions I asked in this chapter. Lay before the Spirit of God your calling, your vision, your passion, your gifts, your character, your pride, your fears, your interior issues, your pace, and your heart. Let God reveal the truth about your life. Then take whatever steps you need to take to become proficient at the single most important aspect of leadership: self-leadership.

CHAPTER TEN

A Leader's Prayer

*"God, Mold and Shape Me to My
Full Leadership Potential"*

Some of the richest times I've spent with God have occurred when I've been alone on a boat. One day, anchored off the Lake Michigan shore, I began journaling some thoughts about my own leadership potential. I wrote, "God, I want to be a better leader than I am. I don't want to stand before you someday and have to admit that I squandered the opportunities you gave me. I want to develop my leadership skills to the peak of my potential. But I need your help. Please direct my growth and instruct me in the way I should go."

As I was writing this prayer, I felt led by the Holy Spirit to scroll through the lives of some of my favorite leaders in the Old and New Testaments. After reflecting on the lives of these diverse men and women, and identifying the praiseworthy components of their leadership, I began to pray that their strengths would find greater expression in my life.

"GOD, MAKE ME LIKE DAVID"

The first leader who came to mind was King David. One reason he is one of my all-time favorite leaders is his optimism. That day on the boat I prayed, "Oh God, give me David's optimism. I need David's capacity to perceive what might happen when you are in the mix."

From the first day David put on the mantle of leadership, his faith-based optimism moved him to attempt feats for God that more cautious leaders would never have considered. David believed so deeply in the power of God that a giant could not intimidate him, a murderous king could not paralyze him, and genocidal enemies could not defeat him. With confidence David marched in whatever direction God pointed him, fully expecting grace and power to be revealed along the way.

Oh, God, I thought, *I need more of that as I lead.*

Even at his lowest point, David's faith-based optimism was strong. When he failed morally with Bathsheba and God struck their firstborn son with illness, David did not give up his optimism. Even though God had said that the child's life would be required for the father's sins, David clung to hope. He fell on his face. He fasted and prayed for six days and nights. He could not let go of the slight possibility that God might spare his newborn son.

But as you know, God did not spare his son. The infant died.

Later, when asked why he'd fasted and prayed, David said, "I thought, 'Who knows? The Lord may be gracious to me and let the child live'" (2 Samuel 12:22). David's optimistic heart beat so strongly in those words.

"Who knows? God might be merciful."

"Who knows? God might use his power on my behalf."

"Who knows? God might surprise me with something supernatural."

Optimists expect to experience God's greatness and love, even when they're facing bleak circumstances.

I need that kind of optimism in my leadership. Don't we all?

The people we lead need to see that kind of optimism in us as well. They get fire-hosed with a steady stream of pessimism every day. Whether it's from television, newspapers, magazines, or crime reports, they hear the same persistent drone: "Things are dark and getting darker. There's no sign of light on the horizon. There's no reason for hope."

People need to hear a leader with faith-based convictions say, "Wait a minute. Things can get better. Human lives can be transformed by the power of Christ. Suffering can be relieved by God's mercy. Oppression can be lifted. Sin can be defeated. The church can push back the gates of hell."

In the aftermath of September 11 and the ensuing recession, I have prayed every day: "God, give me David's optimism. Help me to remember that you are alive, powerful, gracious, and merciful. Help me to believe beyond the shadow of a doubt that you are ready, willing, and able to move in a new way in my life, in your church, and in the world.

"Make me like David, so I can be a leader who inspires hope. Help me lift other people into a faith-based optimism. If ever I, and the people I lead, have needed the positive spirit of David, it's now."

Do you need to pray that prayer?

"GOD, MAKE ME LIKE JONATHAN"

IT WAS NATURAL, AFTER considering David, to scroll through the Scriptures to David's good friend, Jonathan. Because Jonathan's father was King Saul, Jonathan was heir apparent to the throne. He was also a very bright and gifted young leader. But Jonathan's position in life was not as impressive as the condition of his heart. When I thought of Jonathan I prayed, "God, give me Jonathan's capacity to love."

Jonathan had a huge capacity to love. In their youth, David was the recipient of Jonathan's genuine love even though Jonathan could have viewed David as a threat to his own inheritance. But Jonathan never sacrificed his relationship with David to protect his own future. On the contrary, he put his heart on a platter and offered it to David.

That day in my boat I prayed, "God I don't want to be a leader who sacrifices community on the altar of kingdom cause. I don't want to use people. I don't want to see people as tools. I want to have a heart like Jonathan's, with an enormous capacity to love." With a heart like Jonathan's, I'll never again have to worry about having a shrinking heart like I described in the previous chapter.

From time to time I have to remind myself that Jesus taught that the acid test of our discipleship is the test of love. The measuring rod by which my life and leadership will ultimately be assessed is that of love. When I'm thinking clearly, I realize that I'd rather be known for being a man of love than a man of vision. I'd rather be thought of as a man of love than a man of strategic intent. I'd rather be remembered as a man of love than someone who achieved a lot of goals.

That day I began praying earnestly, "God give me Jonathan's capacity to love."

"GOD, MAKE ME LIKE JOSEPH"

AS I CONTINUED PRAYING my mind drifted to Joseph. Joseph is a hero of mine because of his integrity. I prayed, "God give me Joseph's personal holiness."

Joseph's rise to power and influence can only be described as meteoric. Such an ascent often leads to pride and to the assumption that one is an exception to the rules. We all know that power tends to corrupt. As a leader, you may already have felt its corrupting claws in your own flesh.

But Joseph remained uncorrupted by power. From what Scripture tells us, he avoided financial impropriety, political scandal, and sexual seduction. He stayed unstained to the end.

What was the key to Joseph's integrity? I believe he saw his leadership as a holy stewardship for which he would someday stand accountable to God. I believe Joseph lived with the daily awareness that leaders must possess a high degree of moral authority if they're going to lead well. Moral authority comes from a completely surrendered heart, an unsoiled mind, and a clean conscience before God. Joseph had the kind of integrity that led to moral authority and he kept it throughout his entire lifetime.

I need that kind of integrity. People who follow my leadership need to have confidence that I'm not going to wind up in a ditch; that I'm not going to lead a double life; that I'm not going to play with the cash register; that I'm not going to sell out to the values of the world; that I'm not going to be seduced by temptations. People need confidence in my integrity.

But I know that the only way to keep from sliding into depravity is to lay myself before God each and every day of my life and pray for his enabling power.

I'm reminded of an old hymn that describes my life more than I wish it did:

> Prone to wander, Lord I feel it.
> Prone to leave the God I love.[1]

I hate that wandering, rebellious spirit that surfaces in me from time to time. But I can't ignore it or just refuse to address it. It's there and it's real and I have to acknowledge it. Then I have to fight it with a whole array of spiritual practices. These practices can, I confess, become burdensome. But I know their value, so I hang onto them like a drowning man hangs onto a life preserver.

I need the daily discipline of writing out my prayers in long hand in order to stay focused. God bless you if you don't need that tedious discipline, but I do.

I need the daily discipline of solitude so I can listen to God even though the demands of my day scream out to me like wounded animals.

---

[1] "Come, Thou Fount of Every Blessing" by John Wyeth and Robert Robinson.

I need the discipline of being accountable to the people in my life who have the courage to tell me the hard words I need to hear.

Because so much of my life is spent in front of cameras and lights, I need to do secret acts of service on a regular basis and promise God and myself that these good deeds won't find their way into sermon illustrations.

Every leader must figure out what rigors, practices, and spiritual disciplines are necessary for overcoming his or her proneness to wandering. And it's a waste of time for leaders to compare their spiritual regimens with anyone else's. Every leader's routine needs to be custom designed.

That day I prayed, "Oh God, I want to finish my assignment like Joseph finished his, without bringing reproach on you. Please give me the integrity of Joseph."

I believe that a lot of leaders need to pray that prayer. Do you?

"GOD, MAKE ME LIKE JOSHUA"

NEXT I PRAYED, "God, give me Joshua's decisiveness." In my opinion, Joshua's finest moment was when he stood in front of his people and cried, "Choose this day whom you will serve. As for me and my house, we will serve the Lord" (Joshua 24:15).

So much of leadership is about making right decisions and calling others to make them as well. Leaders must come to absolute certainty regarding major life issues, then call the people they lead to do the same.

Joshua did that.

If Joshua were leading your church or mine, he'd cast a God-honoring vision for the future, and then he'd say, "Okay, you've heard the plan. Now it's decision time. You need to either get on board or stand clear because this train is leaving the station."

If Joshua were leading your church or mine, at the close of every salvation message he'd say, "Seekers, sooner or later you have to decide. Are you going to admit your sin and receive grace? Or are you going to walk away from the greatest act of love ever demonstrated to this sin-stained world? You've got to make up your mind. You've got to choose."

Joshua would ask our people to make bold decisions about matters of membership, volunteerism, small group involvement, stewardship, and conflict-resolution. Joshua believed that nobody ever drifts in a God-honoring direction; people have to choose to follow God. I believe that too. People have to make calculated decisions; they have to make tough, often costly, choices. And leaders are often the catalysts for those heroic decisions.

More and more we leaders must take responsibility for leading people to decision points concerning important life issues. We must remind people that life is not a game nor is spiritual growth something to be taken lightly. The issues around which our lives and ministries revolve are eternal, and, therefore, worthy of some bold decisions.

As I thought about Joshua that day out on the boat, I prayed, "God, give me Joshua's decisiveness. I need it!" Maybe you need it too.

"GOD, MAKE ME LIKE ESTHER"

REMEMBER THIS REMARKABLE YOUNG woman? After reflecting on her story I prayed, "Oh God, give me Esther's courage."

Thrust into leadership more because of her beauty than her skills, Esther wound up at the crossroads of her people's destiny—and her own. She could either risk her life by pleading her people's case before a dangerous king, or she could protect her position and walk away from the crisis at hand. Do you recall what she did? After asking the entire local Jewish community to fast and pray for her for three days and nights, she said, "When this is done, I will go to the king, even though it is against the law. And if I perish, I perish" (Esther 4:16).

"I will do the right thing . . . and if I perish, I perish." Esther put it all on the line. She was willing to lose status, position, perks, security, even her life, to do what God had called her to do.

"If I perish, I perish."

Her courage wasn't a manifestation of reckless insanity, and obviously it wasn't the result of excess testosterone. Esther simply believed that certain values were worth living—and dying—for.

Sometimes when I look at the weakened condition of the church worldwide, I find myself thinking that for church renewal to occur, a whole generation of leaders is going to have to manifest the courage of Esther. They're going to have to say, "Enough. It's a new day. There's a new reality out there. We're going to have to do church a new way—a more biblical, relevant, thoughtful, and creative way than we've ever done it before. If in the attempt we lose our reputations, our status, or our security, so be it. We've got to do what God has called us to do—and if we perish, we perish."

Sometimes I ache when I see the enormous potential for church renewal that is unrealized for lack of leadership courage. Sometimes I have to fight off the urge to grab the lapels of leaders and ask, "When are you going to make your mark? What lifetime are you waiting for? In which reincarnation will you finally do what God has gifted you to do? When are you going to start leading courageously?"

Sometimes I feel like pleading with pastors. "Will you please either act decisively or step aside so someone else can? Do one or the other. But someone has to lead this church with courage."

I hope I'm not sounding superior when I say this. You would be shocked to learn how often in my prayers I have to confess old-fashioned gutlessness and cowardliness. I shudder to think how much woe I've caused Willow because I have lacked what a youthful beauty queen had lots of—courage!

Too often I hesitate to take courageous action because I don't want to put decades of work on the line. Sometimes I say to myself,

"I've taken enough hits. I don't want to take any more risks. I don't want to expend myself to the limits one more time."

But when I feel this way, I try to remember Esther, who said, "I'll do the right thing . . . and if I perish, I perish."

I need Esther's courage. Lots of us leaders do.

"GOD, MAKE ME LIKE SOLOMON"

As I CONTINUED REFLECTING on different leaders, I thought of Solomon and his legendary wisdom and I prayed, "Oh God, if you would just grant me a portion of Solomon's wisdom."

If you were to peel back the confident veneer of most leaders, you'd find men and women who often lay sleepless in their beds at night, tossing and turning with uncertainty. Questions without easy answers haunt them: Is it time to move forward with a new plan or time to consolidate and let the dust settle for awhile? Is it time to inspire the congregation or time to bring a word of rebuke? Is it time to give a new staff member opportunity to prove himself or is it time to help him find a new place to serve?

Occasionally people graciously ask how they can pray for me. My response is the same almost every time: "Please pray that I will have wisdom. Please pray that my leadership will be characterized by a godly sober-mindedness. Please pray that I will discern God's mind on every matter."

Each year I am increasingly sobered by the tragic implications of my leading Willow or the Willow Creek Association off course. People look to leaders to set direction. How can we choose the right course apart from God's wisdom?

I desperately need Solomon's wisdom. You do too.

"GOD, MAKE ME LIKE JEREMIAH"

NEXT I THOUGHT OF Jeremiah's emotional authenticity. When his ministry was not going well Jeremiah poured out his disappointment to God. When charts were headed the wrong way, when people were unresponsive to his teaching, when the evil one seemed to be gaining the upper hand, Jeremiah didn't get cynical, nor did he slide into bitterness. With rare honestly, he expressed his true feelings to God. He admitted that he felt abandoned and fearful of the future. Then he let God restore his broken heart.

According to human score cards, Jeremiah's ministry never went well during his entire lifetime. But he stayed faithful to his calling. He didn't deny his disappointments, but because he turned to God honestly in the midst of them and opened his heart to divine strength and encouragement, he was able to move from despair to hope. Despite the disappointments and thwarted expectations in his life and ministry, he never lost his confidence in the faithfulness of God. In Lamentations 3:22b–23 he wrote fourteen unforgettable words about God. "For [your] compassions never fail. They are new every morning; great is your faithfulness."

I used to be pretty good at putting on a "game face." When ministry got hard or life got disappointing, I knew what words I had to say and how wide I had to smile to convince people that everything was okay. But over time I realized that sometimes it was easier to convince other people that everything was fine than it was to convince my own heart. I learned that the kind of hope and confidence in God that characterized Jeremiah has nothing to do with putting on a game face. It only comes to those who spill out the truth of their broken heart to God and let him touch them with healing balm.

I wonder how many of us need to pray, "God, give me the emotional authenticity of Jeremiah," so we can experience the authentic faithfulness of God.

"GOD, MAKE ME LIKE NEHEMIAH"

NEHEMIAH IS ONE OF the greatest leaders in the Old Testament. While Nehemiah's leadership has much to teach us, what I most needed to learn from him was his commitment to celebration.

You know the story. After fifty-two days of nonstop rebuilding of Jerusalem's walls, Nehemiah arranged a huge celebration for all his faithful workers. He wanted them to savor their collective achievement. He wanted them to honor each other's hard work and to praise God for sustaining them during their heroic construction efforts. Scripture describes in great detail just how good this particular party was.

Nehemiah raised the bar for me when it comes to celebration. He reminded me that all work and no play makes for dull people and dull churches. All service and no celebration is a formula for wearing people down and draining their joy. We leaders must not let that happen. We need to be as intentional in planning the victory parties as we are at setting and achieving the organizational goals.

One way for leaders to keep up the morale of those they lead is to punctuate long seasons of serving with raucous, soul-lifting, God-honoring celebrations. I prayed out on the boat that day, "God, may I never forget how important parties are. Like Jeremiah, help me remember to celebrate."

We've had some good parties around Willow since that day on the water. It has become a custom among our ministry teams to finish every major conference with a festive, celebratory event that reminds us what a privilege it is to do what we do and to do it with people we love. Sometimes we take over whole restaurants, enjoying wonderful food and drink until late into the night. We laugh as we tell behind-the-scene stories. We remind each other of God's incredible grace in helping us through major challenges and unexpected problems. We encourage and thank each other for our varied contributions. In the midst of all this wonderful esprit de corps the rigors of ministry suddenly seem light.

Leaders, have you planned any parties lately?

"GOD, MAKE ME LIKE PETER"

AFTER THINKING ABOUT NEHEMIAH, my mind crossed into the New Testament to Peter. Scripture covers the good, the bad, and the ugly aspects of Peter's leadership. While there's much in Peter we leaders need to avoid, there's also a lot to be admired. When I think of Peter's willingness to step out and take action I pray, "God, make me the kind of leader who knows how important it is to take initiative."

Even though Peter takes heat for becoming fearful and sinking when he tried to walk on the water, shouldn't he at least get credit for being the *only* disciple to get out of the boat? That took initiative.

And yes, it's true Peter made verbal commitments he couldn't always keep. But sometimes he was the *only* one of the twelve willing to speak up at all. He was the first to publicly identify Jesus as the long-awaited Messiah. He took initiative in honoring the Lord with that title.

And of course, we all know he got a little carried away in Gethsemane and whacked off a guy's ear. But Peter couldn't sit idly by and do nothing while his Savior and friend was falsely arrested. He had to do *something!*

As much of an activist as I am, I still resist taking initiative from time to time. And I watch other church leaders do the same. We hide out in our offices while our churches drift or decline. Or we sit in coffee shops analyzing and criticizing other leaders who are out in front taking risks. Sure, they might be fouling up once in a while, but at least they are trying to make a difference. How much better that we, like Peter, join the ones who are initiating kingdom action, trying something new, and launching out in ways that keep the enemy on his heels.

How much better if we would all pray for the initiative-taking boldness of Peter.

"GOD, MAKE ME LIKE PAUL"

AND FINALLY THAT DAY, how could I not pray a short prayer about the leadership of the apostle Paul? When I thought of Paul I prayed, "God give me Paul's intensity."

Chicagoans have an enormous advantage when it comes to understanding the concept of intensity. For years we had front row seats for watching one of the most remarkable athletes in the history of professional sports: Michael Jordan. The legacy he left Chicago goes far beyond his outstanding talent or his amazing athleticism. What set him far above other talented professional athletes was Michael's unbelievable intensity. His focus. His work ethic. His competitiveness. His drive to win.

Michael's intensity was so powerful that it lifted all of his teammates to a higher level. Often as the game wore on, you could watch the opposing team start to wither and to melt under the pressure of Michael's incessant drive. Late in the fourth quarter Michael would just take over. His message was clear: "I will not be denied. This team will not give up the victory." Usually the other teams ended up not only defeated, but demoralized as well.

The apostle Paul is the only Christ follower I've ever known whose intensity about Jesus could match Michael Jordan's intensity about basketball. When you read the story of the apostle Paul the intensity of his commitment is so obvious:

- "I do not consider my life as dear unto myself. Only that I would achieve the mission that I have received from the Lord." (Acts 20:24)
- "One thing I do ... I press toward the mark for the prize of the high calling of God in Christ Jesus." (Philippians 3:13, 14)
- "I will gladly spend and be completely spent for the sake of the church." (2 Corinthians 12:15)
- "For me to live is Christ, to die is gain." (Philippians 1:21)
- "In a race there is only one winner. When I run a race I do so to win." (1 Corinthians 9:24)
- And then his famous words near the end of his life, "I have fought the good fight, I finished the race, I have kept the faith." (2 Timothy 4:7–8)

- And finally he directs his words to Christ followers for centuries to come: "There is a crown waiting for me—and not for me only, but for you too." (2 Timothy 4:8b)

Fight! Keep the faith! Finish! When I hear those words from Paul I can barely contain my emotions. I want more of that intensity in my life. On the boat that day I prayed, "God, help me stay focused. Help me keep my eyes on the prize of the high calling of God in Christ Jesus. Help me run the most important race in the world with all the energy I can muster. Help me to win it for the glory of the One I will worship in heaven forever. Help me get to the end of my life knowing I fought the good fight with every ounce of strength I possessed; that I finished the ministry that was entrusted to me; that I kept the faith and never compromised."

My heart's desire is to pursue an imperishable wreath with the same intensity that Michael Jordan pursues a perishable one. The stakes of the kingdom are immeasurably higher than the stakes of professional sports. The outcome of our game has eternal significance. The payoff is forever.

I think it's time we all ask God for greater intensity. I'm not talking about frenetic busyness, but about an intelligent, Christ-honoring, apostle Paul-like intensity. How about right now reaching down deep and praying the words of Paul? Repeat them with a kind of leadership resolve. Say them until the words are cemented in your mind.

"I do not consider my life as dear unto myself. Only that I would achieve the mission that I received from the Lord."

"This one thing I do: I press toward the mark for the prize of the high calling of God in Christ Jesus."

"I will gladly spend and be spent for the sake of the church."

"For me to live is Christ and to die is gain."

"In a race there is only one winner. When I run a race I do so to win."

"I have fought the good fight. I have finished the course. I have kept the faith."

"Oh God, make me like Paul. Give me his intensity so I will have the power of your Holy Spirit, strength in the middle of the battle and courage to endure."

May our prayers shape us, and may God's grace lift us to our full leadership potential.

CHAPTER ELEVEN

The Leader's Pathway

A Vital Walk with God

How important is the supernatural component of leadership, the "God part"? Beyond the gift of leadership, beyond the skills and talents required, beyond the decades of experience, is there anything more that we as leaders need? Is it *really* all that important for leaders to walk in vital union with Jesus Christ?

Examining 1 Corinthians 13 against the backdrop of this query reveals an interesting perspective:

> If I cast vision with the tongues of men and angels,
>   but lead without the love of God at my core,
> I am a ringing cell phone or worse, a clamoring vacuous
>   corporate type.
> If I have the gift of leadership and can provide direction,
>   build teams, and set goals,
>   but fail to exhibit Christ-like kindness or give Christ the
>   credit for my accomplishments,
> In the eyes of God, all my achievements count for precisely
>   nothing.

If I give my salary to the poor, my reserved parking space in
the church lot to a summer intern, or my deacons'
bodies to be burned,
but neglect to relate and work in a manner worthy of the
one whose name I bear,
In the final analysis, it all counts for precisely nothing.
A close, humble walk with Christ never fails. It strengthens
the heart,
redirects the will, restrains the ego, and purifies
the motives.
It never fails.
When I was a young leader, independent and too busy
to pray,
I blew stuff up and wounded every third person I led.
But now that I am mature and have left my childish
ways . . .
I do that somewhat less!
And now these three remain:
the faith to follow God boldly,
the hope to press on even when my heart
is breaking,
and the love to enrich the hearts of all those I lead.
But the greatest of these is love—the love that only comes
from a quiet, close, daily walk with Christ.

A LEADER'S GREATEST GIFT: A FULLY YIELDED HEART

WE ARE ALL FAMILIAR with Jesus' words from John 15:5: "I am the
vine; you are the branches. If you remain in me and I in you, you
will bear much fruit." His promise reminds us that if we stay in
close connection with him, he will infuse our leadership with
power, creativity, courage, and whatever else it takes for us to bear
fruit for the glory of God. But still I meet church leaders all over the
world who admit to me privately, in hushed tones, that they have

never been able to establish and sustain a close, consistent, vital walk with Jesus Christ.

They tell me how ashamed they feel when other leaders describe their consistent practice of disciplines like solitude, fasting, prayer, journaling, or Scripture memorization. Leaders often end their private confessions of inadequacy by asking, "Is there something wrong with me? Do I have a character flaw or spiritual defect? Why can't I establish and sustain a vital walk with Christ?"

Often I suggest that perhaps they have never discovered their spiritual pathway—their unique means of moving toward vital union with Christ.

Years ago I began to notice that various leaders whom I respected went about their walks with God in vastly different ways. The variety was stunning to me. I started keeping a mental list of all their different approaches. Then I came across a book called *Sacred Pathways,* written by Gary Thomas, which further pushed my thinking on this subject. I would strongly recommend that all leaders make a place in their library for this profound and helpful book.

Sacred pathways are like doors that open into a room where we can feel particularly close to God. Just as different leaders have many different personalities and combinations of gifts, so they have many different spiritual pathways. In this chapter I want to discuss a number of these pathways, hoping that leaders will identify their own particular pathway, and in so doing revitalize their own walk with God.

THE RELATIONAL PATHWAY

HAVE YOU EVER NOTICED how difficult it is for some people to flourish in their walk with Christ when they attempt to do it alone?

For these people, solitude feels like solitary confinement. It frustrates them. It feels suffocating. Bible studies done in isolation seem to them like empty homework assignments and produce very little growth. Sitting alone at a worship service is enough to ruin the entire experience and serving alone is a fate worse than death. People who connect best with God on the relational pathway feel a kind of spiritual dullness when they try to walk with God alone.

But inject a strong dose of relationship into their pursuit of God and watch what happens! Almost immediately these individuals begin to thrive spiritually. When they pray with a group of people, they can almost feel the presence of God physically. When they study the Bible with other fired-up Christ followers, they come away enriched and impassioned. When they work together with a team, serving is one of the greatest joys in their life. When they praise God publicly with other believers, their worship becomes twice as meaningful.

It's obvious. Their primary pathway to God is relational. When leaders with the relational pathway acknowledge it and lean into it, they begin to flourish spiritually in ways they never could have if they'd attempted to go it alone.

My guess is that many leaders fit this profile. What would happen if such leaders designed their personal spiritual formation plans around this reality?

I know a pastor who used to beat himself up mercilessly for not spending enough time in solitude. Strange thing though, whenever he did manage to be alone for long periods of time, he became brooding and morose. Dark thoughts filled his mind. Though he engaged in solitude to make himself available to God, the experience never failed to set him back spiritually.

Some time ago I suggested that he might solve his problem by taking two or three guys with him on his spiritual retreats. The look on his face said it all: Would that be legal? Would it qualify as a spiritual retreat? He'd been convinced that the true test of spirituality was the ability to engage in long periods of solitude. But in his case, that formula was a setup for spiritual frustration because his pathway is primarily relational. Now that he's inviting others to join him on his spiritual retreats, he is growing like a weed and encouraging others in their spiritual growth as well.

What a blessing that leader would have missed had he continued shaming himself because he wasn't good at solitude. On the relational pathway, he is discovering the closeness with God that he had always longed for.

THE INTELLECTUAL PATHWAY

PEOPLE WHO THRIVE ON the intellectual pathway are those whose minds must be fully engaged before they can make significant spiritual progress. When these folks sit in testimonial services where people are passionately describing God's amazing activity in their lives, they find themselves thinking, *Where's the beef? These heartwarming stories are all well and good, but where's the substance? Where's the theological data? I need something to chew on. I'm dying here!*

These people can't have their morning devotions without two or three opened commentaries flanking their Bibles. They carry several intellectually stretching books with them wherever they go. They gravitate toward classes, seminars, and special events that will challenge their thinking. Why? Because they know that their hearts will never fully engage until their minds are filled with truth.

But when that happens, there is no stopping these folks! When Martin Luther realized the truth of the gospel, when John Calvin grasped the doctrine of the sovereignty of God, when Chuck Colson fully comprehended the intellectual supremacy of a Christian worldview—*nothing* stopped them.

For people wired up this way, once their minds are fully convinced, their hearts and will quickly follow and their convictions are rock solid. I think it is quite possible that the apostle Paul had an intellectual pathway. For him, the transformation of the world depended on the "renewing of our minds" (Romans 12:2). Paul was quick to appeal to the rational side of human nature, apparently convinced that once a person's mind belonged to God, everything else would follow. Win the intellectual argument, and it would be game, set, match. Victory!

I've met many leaders who feel guilty about their intellectual proclivities. They don't want anybody knowing that they sneak peeks at the deep stuff once in a while. They feel "unleaderly" if they spend too much time in research and study. The truth of the matter is that if they don't keep their minds challenged, they will probably dry up spiritually.

Teacher and author Lee Strobel comes to mind when I think of a leader with an intellectual pathway. He researched Christianity for two solid years before he could bow the knee to Christ. His mind needed to be convinced before he could open his heart. Now, years after his conversion, he reads theology, archaeology, philosophy, and history recreationally. It feeds his soul.

When Lee worked on my staff, he would burst into my office bubbling over with enthusiasm because some archaeologist somewhere in the Middle East had made a discovery that Lee thought would force every skeptic to his knees. "The evidence is overwhelming!" he'd shout. "How can anybody with a brain believe otherwise?"

I'd just smile.

But I think the day Lee stops stretching himself intellectually will be the day his spiritual life begins to fade. That's what the intellectual pathway is all about.

If you have an intellectual orientation like Lee, stop apologizing for it and start developing a spiritual formation plan that focuses on the development of your mind. Love God with all your *mind* and watch what happens to your daily union with him.

THE SERVING PATHWAY

SOME FOLKS CAN'T SEEM to catch their spiritual stride and feel consistently close to God unless they're quietly and consistently laboring in kingdom vineyards. When it comes to thinkers and doers, these people are the doers.

They read their Bibles, pray, and attend worship services like the rest of us. But if you ask them when they feel closest to God or when they feel most dialed in, centered, joyful, and alive in Christ, don't expect them to answer, "During prayer," or, "When I'm studying theology," or, "When I'm singing a worship song." If they are honest they will answer, "When I'm serving. When I'm volunteering in ministry. When I know I'm helping to accomplish the work of God."

One of our board members at Willow has a serving pathway. Serving is so central to his walk with God that he took an early retirement and relocated his home right across the street from the church. Every week he spends several days volunteering on campus. If you ask him why he does it he just breaks out in a smile and says, "Because I never feel as close to God as when I'm an instrument in his hands serving others in the kingdom."

At a recent baptism service, I saw him sitting in the crowd, crying his eyes out at the sight of hundreds of freshly redeemed people. He knew his serving had played a part in the overall redemptive scheme. If you took serving away from him, you'd close the door on his pathway to God.

If you're someone who feels closest to God when you are doing something for him, then lean into the serving pathway. Put together a spiritual formation plan that centers on serving, and I predict that your awareness of God's presence will increase dramatically.

THE CONTEMPLATIVE PATHWAY

THROUGHOUT CHURCH HISTORY THERE have always been some Christians who feel like they're marching to a different drummer. While other believers are joyfully filling their calendars with relational commitments or serving opportunities, these sincere Christians are carefully guarding their schedules, avoiding at all costs the patterns of busyness they see around them. For reasons they may not fully understand, these people are easily drained by relationships and activities. But they can spend almost unlimited time in solitude. Give them a Bible, a good piece of literature, a poem and a journal, and they'll disappear for days.

These people thrive on the contemplative pathway. For them, just being alone with God is enough. They spend hours reflecting on the goodness of God and have an enormous capacity for prayer and private worship. They operate with sensitive spiritual antennae and can discern the activity of God wherever they are.

But the downside to this wonderful pathway is that sometimes contemplatives feel out of step with the rest of the Christian community. Their sensitivity causes them to take very seriously things that other people don't. They observe beauty in the natural realm and wonder how others in the Christian community can walk right past without even breaking stride. They often serve as the conscience of the faith community, calling us to ministries of compassion and inclusiveness. They reflect on the numbers of people suffering in the world and wonder why so few people care. Often idealistic, they help us focus on what kingdom life is supposed to be like.

Contemplatives also tend to have rich inner worlds. They can at times seem scattered, but often in reality they're incubating creative ideas. Though these folks may seem a little out of step with the rest of us, they're the ones who compose the songs that stir our hearts or write the books that make us think new thoughts about God.

If you know contemplative types, relate to them very carefully. Immature leaders usually think that contemplatives are wasting time with all their deep thinking. "Get busy!" they want to say. "There's a hill to take. Let's go." But mature leaders understand that contemplatives need to spend considerable time outside the mainstream. They need to protect their thought life. Eventually their reflections will lead to something wonderful that will bless the whole church.

Leaders whose primary pathway is contemplative need to give themselves an extra measure of grace. They need to give themselves permission to spend long hours in quiet reflection, even if others view it as inappropriate or strange, because for them that's the door that opens into the presence of God.

THE ACTIVIST PATHWAY

UNLIKE CONTEMPLATIVES, ACTIVISTS ARE at their best at a speed of Mach 2. They're happiest when white knuckled and gasping for breath. Because of their wiring they need—actually they *revel* in—a highly challenging environment that pushes them to the absolute edge of their potential. It's when they're right on that edge that they feel closest to God. In fact, they feel so close to God that they invoke his name with great sincerity, "Oh, God! Oh, God! Oh, God!"

Other people tend to fear for those on the activist pathway. It seems as though these activists are consistently biting off more kingdom work than they can chew. Casual onlookers start to feel sorry for them. They might even attempt to bail them out until they realize that activists *like* to live this way.

Christian activists choose a fast pace. No one has a gun to their heads. No third party stuffed a rocket in their britches and lit the fuse. They're not victims. They *love* riding rockets. Put them on an Amtrak train and they'll figure out a way to double its speed.

Do you think God made a mistake when he wired some leaders this way? Be careful. The church of Jesus Christ wouldn't be what it is today without some of these characters in her past. Read about John Wesley. The guy was a ministry maniac. Learn about George Whitefield. He preached himself into near exhaustion throughout the course of his life. Then there was D. L. Moody, who kept all his associates wondering how one person could do all he did.

Scores of such men and women received a calling from God, burst out of the starting blocks, and ran full speed from the day they received their orders until the day they keeled over and died. Along the way they ignited all kinds of kingdom activity. Ask activists when they feel closest to God and they will respond, "When I'm way out on a limb of faith flapping in the breeze. When the battle against evil is the fiercest and the only hope for victory is divine intervention." Activists are fond of saying, "I feel closest to God when I have wrung out every last drop of my emotional, physical, and spiritual potential for a worthy kingdom cause. Or when I collapse on the pillow at night and say, 'There God—I gave you my all, my best, my very last drop.'"

That's as good as it gets for activists. I know a little about this because this is my primary pathway. (Surprise! Surprise!) Believe me, I'm not advocating insanity. I've done insanity. It's highly overrated. But some activists feel guilty about the extraordinary energy with which they attack ministry. My counsel to them is to accept that God made them that way and to lean into their pathway. Come into God's presence—even if it's with your hair on fire. He knows our kind and enjoys us completely. Really!

THE CREATION PATHWAY

NOW LET'S TAKE A look at people who tend to grow best and relate to God most closely when they're surrounded by nature. These people are the naturalists, the tree huggers, the green believers. They come alive from head to toe whenever they are surrounded by natural splendor, be it mountains, deserts, plains, woods, oceans, or beaches.

For these people, being in a natural environment dramatically increases their awareness of God. They often draw direct spiritual meaning from nature. People who love the mountains, for example, see in the massive rock formations a reflection of the rock-solid faithfulness of God or a manifestation of his unchanging character. Desert-loving folks might hike in the heat of the mid-day sun to an oasis that offers shade, water, and refreshment. There they find spiritual comfort and refreshment because they are reminded of the promise of God to restore our dry, dusty souls.

Ask people with a strong creation pathway when they feel closest to God, and it's a no-brainer for them. Ask them where they would prefer to have their devotions, where they would most enjoy being with a small group of brothers and sisters, where they would most like to reflect for a while on their life, and they'll answer, "Close to nature." We shouldn't find this all that surprising, given that God created man and woman and put them in a garden. So it's just back to their original roots for these folks.

Imagine what would happen if someone who was wired up like this actually put together a spiritual formation plan that allowed them to triple the amount of time they spend in nature. What if they moved to a different location so they could live more closely to the natural world God created? What if they included nature in their vacation plans, knowing that by doing so they would rest and refresh not only their bodies but their souls as well? I believe that such a plan would almost guarantee people on the creation pathway a greater awareness of the presence of God in their lives.

THE WORSHIP PATHWAY

IN RECENT YEARS I'VE become friends with a business leader from another state. Though he's been a Christian since childhood, he really didn't understand worship until a few years ago. He had attended the same church most of his adult life, but the whole twenty-year experience had left him feeling empty. He'd grown in knowledge from the teaching at his church, but despite having a full head he had an empty heart.

One Sunday a friend invited him to visit a church on the other side of town. The friend's church was one that worshiped "in the spirit." Actually, they worshiped with a *lot* of spirit! My hard-core businessman friend experienced a strange phenomenon at that church. For the first several weeks he bawled like a baby throughout the entire worship service. He had no clue what was happening to him. He thought maybe he'd blown a midlife gasket.

But eventually it started making sense to him. He concluded that his heart had been so starved for God-honoring worship that when he finally experienced it, it was like a dam broke inside of him and a new wave of the Holy Spirit's activity flooded his life.

Eventually he joined a church like the one he had visited with his friend. He had to. And these days, whenever he has a yearning to feel the presence of God, whenever he has a big marketplace decision to make and wants to be sure he gets it right, or whenever he has a full heart and wants to let it overflow in praise to God he takes a half dozen worship CDs and goes for a long drive in his car. Occasionally he ends up pulling over to the side of the road because the presence of God so completely overwhelms him that he can no longer drive. Worship is without a doubt his primary pathway to God.

I think I could present a case that David, the author of many of the Psalms, was someone whose primary pathway to God was worship. Remember what he wrote?

> Bless the Lord, O my soul,
>   and all that is within me.
> Bless the Lord and may I not forget
>   a single one of his benefits.
> He redeems my life from destruction.
> He crowns me with loving-kindness.
> He satisfies my life with good things.
> Bless the Lord you angels.
> Bless the Lord all you his host.
> Bless the Lord all the works of his.
> Let everything that has life and breath praise the Lord.
> Praise the Lord!
>
> —Psalm 103:1–5b, 20–21; 150:6

I think David felt closest to God and most fully alive when he was worshiping. Many church leaders, like David, have this worship pathway. If they are wise they will design a spiritual formation plan that allows them to delve often into the spirit of worship.

Now that you have some ideas about spiritual pathways, what can you do to move more consistently along your own pathway?

FIRST, IDENTIFY YOUR PATHWAY

I'VE LISTED SEVEN PATHWAYS but this list is more representative than exhaustive. Gary Thomas lists several others in his book, *Sacred Pathways,* and also discusses various nuances of those I mentioned that many be helpful to some readers. My guess is that you have probably been trying to identify the spiritual pathway that best fits you. It's certainly possible to be inclined toward more than one, but most people have a primary pathway. A word of caution though: Resist the temptation to compare your pathway with other peoples' pathways. Also resist the temptation to identify the pathway you wish were true about you. I call that pathway envy.

When I first read Thomas's book, I knew the activist pathway described me hands down. But instead of being excited, I was disappointed. Like many people throughout the centuries, I considered the real heavyweights of the kingdom to be the contemplatives. They're the ones who think and write the deep stuff. I thought to myself, *I'm going to have to spend the rest of my life lumped in with the kingdom maniacs. Why couldn't I be more like the truly spiritual guys—Henri Nouwen, Thomas Merton, St. John of the Cross?* (I know about these guys because my contemplative wife reads them all the time.)

The more I thought about it, though, the more I sensed God saying to me, "Quit thinking like that, Bill. If I'd wanted you to be wired up like a classic contemplative, I would have wired you that way. But I didn't." Deep down I knew that. I'm no monk. I'm never going to become a desert father. I'd rather fly over the desert at

Mach 2, get to my destination, and challenge church leaders to get off their rears and lead.

Then I want to fly back to Willow and challenge seekers to get off their rears and get into the kingdom. And then I want to challenge believers to get off their rears and get into the action. I might as well accept it: I'm no monk. Desert fathers probably wouldn't even use the word "rear." They probably didn't even have rears, they fasted so much.

Oh well, that's just who I am. And you are just who you are. So let's all make a deal not to compare ourselves to each other or to stuff ourselves into preconceived molds. Let's just accept the particular pathway that brings us close to God and be thankful for it.

SECOND, LEAN INTO YOUR PATHWAY

EXPERIMENT WITH IT. TRY it on for size. If the relational pathway ushers you into new levels of spiritual growth, have at it. Fill your life with the kinds of friendships and activities that help you grow.

If serving helps you feel close to God, if intellectual stimulation feeds your soul, or if any of the other pathways help you focus more clearly on God—practice it! As you do so, you will find yourself establishing and maintaining a deeper walk with God than you've ever known before.

THIRD, APPRECIATE ALL THE PATHWAYS

EXPERIMENT ONCE IN A while with all the various pathways, even though certain ones are a stretch for you. Why? Because they all offer opportunity for growth. People with serving pathways should periodically read intellectually stimulating material because it will enhance their understanding of God. Activist types should quiet themselves and try the contemplative approach from time to time. As foreign as it first seemed to me, I have benefited enormously from this pathway. Contemplatives should occasionally come out of their secluded corners and fellowship and serve with the more relational types. They'd welcome you with open arms. To maximize your spiritual growth, lean into your best way of connecting with God, but then begin to experiment with each of the others.

FINALLY, HELP OTHERS IDENTIFY THEIR PATHWAYS

LEADERS CAN PLAY A vital role in helping people on their teams and in their churches identify their pathways. When those you lead begin to understand that there is at least one pathway that will enable them to relate to Christ more closely, they will thank you for a lifetime.

And imagine the difference it would make if all our leadership teams and volunteers were led by people who were in vital union with Jesus Christ. Imagine the fruit that could be born, the creativity that could flow, the power that could be unleashed, if we were all regularly accessing the presence and power of God through the pathway that he's designed for us. The church would truly become a force that the gates of hell could not hold back!

CHAPTER TWELVE

Developing an
Enduring Spirit

Staying the Course

If YOU COULD ASK YOUR SINGLE MOST PRESSING QUESTION AND WITH a wave of a wand walk away with a solid answer—what would your question be?" That's how I recently started a mentoring session with five highly effective senior pastors.

I was surprised by their responses. I thought these seasoned church leaders would pose questions about building staff, improving preaching and teaching, clarifying mission and values, or raising funds.

But the single most pressing issue for all of these pastors related to enduring. One asked, "How am I going to find the strength to keep going, given the weight of the pressures facing me at church?" Another asked, "Is my life in ministry sustainable over the long haul? Can I do what I'm doing for another twenty-five years?" One joked about timing his burnout just before his crackup.

These leaders at the peak of their ministry careers with years of successful church work behind them were all struggling with the same issue: Am I going to survive my calling? Am I going to make it across the finish line?

I suppose I shouldn't have been surprised by their mutually held concern. For the first eighteen or nineteen years of Willow, sustainability was one of the most pressing concerns in my life as well. I came very close to bailing out of church work many times because I knew, deep in my heart, that I could not continue to live the way I was living over the long haul. What made it worse was that I didn't know how to modify my ministry to make it work—or even if it could work.

I remember thinking to myself, *Why perpetuate this? I mean, if I'm going to crash someday anyway, why not crash now? If I wait, the crash is just going to get more spectacular. And the more spectacular the crash, the more people it's going to damage in the end. So why keep up this insanity?*

AS GOOD AS IT GETS OR IMPENDING DOOM?

WHEN I WAS A BOY, my friends and I would rip the metal wheels off discarded roller skates and attach them to thin boards of plywood. Then we would shoulder these homemade skateboards, walk to the top of the biggest hill in our town, take a deep breath, and jump on.

The first few hundred yards down the hill were about as good as it gets for kids our age. Our screams and war whoops echoed all over the neighborhood. But then we started to gain speed and suddenly things got very quiet. We could no longer ignore the frightening truth: Skateboards don't have brakes. What was coming was inevitable and we all knew it. To avoid killing ourselves, we would have to take a flying leap from our boards. The big question was where we would land—in a patch of grass or on a square of asphalt?

Can you empathize with our junior high dilemma?

We craved the adrenaline rush of speeding faster and faster down the hill, but we were haunted by the knowledge that the higher the speed, the more painful the crash. All the way down the hill we were pulled between two conflicting realities: *Speed is good! Broken bones are bad!*

Some of us made wiser choices than others.

Church leaders understand about conflicting realities. A pastor rolls up his or her sleeves and starts to build a church. Seekers start coming to Christ and soon they're growing up. People start joining small groups, discovering their spiritual gifts, and beginning to serve the poor. All the charts are going up, and that is good and exciting and inspiring. But then the budgets and the buildings start going up, and the pace starts going up, and the pressures and responsibilities and stress levels start going up, up, up.

And you begin to fear that your life is heading out of control. If the speed keeps accelerating, you're going to have to leap. And your landing will probably not be pretty. The formula for crash and burn is becoming clearer to you: The faster you go, the more spectacular the crash. And a more spectacular crash means more damaged people.

If the speed in your life has accelerated to the point that the thrill of serving Christ has been replaced by a sense of impending doom, then join the crowd. Almost every church leader I've known who was really serious about God, who was fully aware of the realities of heaven and hell, who had an authentic love for the bride of Christ, and who really believed that the local church is the hope of the world has wondered how long he or she could hold out before the inevitable "something awful" happened.

Some church leaders become so troubled by a sense of dread concerning their future that they finally ask the pivotal question: Is it possible to survive the rigors of building a prevailing church?

My answer to any church leader asking questions about sustainability in ministry is a resounding yes! If you do it right, you can endure. In fact, you can even flourish. Even you. Even in your situation.

THE GRADUATE SCHOOL OF ENDURANCE

I COULDN'T HAVE ANSWERED questions about endurance with such confidence ten years ago, or even five years ago. But I can shout it from the mountaintops today. I'm thoroughly convinced that God is perfectly capable of helping each of us finish what he has called us to do. And I firmly believe that he will move us beyond enduring to enjoying, beyond surviving to prevailing, if we are willing to do a little learning.

So allow me to enroll you in the graduate school of endurance.

FIRST COURSE: MAKE YOUR CALLING SURE AND STAY FOCUSED

MAKING YOUR CALLING SURE is a 101 class, but if you're going to make it to the end, you must master the material in this class. The objective of the class is to help you sort out exactly what God has asked you to do in this world. This curriculum is based on 2 Timothy 4:5b where the apostle Paul says, "Fulfill your ministry."

Fulfill *your* ministry—nothing more, nothing less.

What does Paul mean when he says, "Fulfill your ministry?" He means fulfill the exact ministry that God *gave you*. Not the ministry you dreamed up during a bout of personal grandiosity. Not the one that makes you feel responsible for the salvation of the entire world. Not the one that forces you out of the basic wiring pattern that God gave you. Not the one that pushes you so far beyond your measure of faith that fear and anxiety dominate your daily life.

Fulfill *your* ministry. The one that flows out of a sincere spirit of humility and submission; the one that matches the exact role God assigned you in the worldwide redemptive drama; the one that corresponds with your true spiritual gifts, passions, and talents; the one that is proportionate to the measure of faith that God has given you.

Fulfill *your* ministry.

Christian leaders I have talked with who have faithfully worn the mantle of ministry for twenty, thirty, sometimes forty years, often attribute their longevity not to any particular things they did but to the many things *they didn't do*. When I congratulate them for having accomplished so much, they are quick to remind me of all that *they didn't accomplish*. "Well," they say, "if you knew all the ministry opportunities I turned down, you probably wouldn't be congratulating me!"

But those leaders are some of the wisest leaders I know. They understand that the key to leadership survival is staying focused. They know that the most valuable asset leaders have is a powerful "No" muscle. And they know that this muscle needs to be flexed every time an opportunity, no matter how noble the cause, threatens to lure them from the task God assigned to them. They have learned how to say, "No, that's not my calling. That's not my assignment. I'm sure heaven has instructed someone to do that, but it's not me."

During a very trying era when I was struggling with being overextended, I put a famous statement on my door: "What part of the word NO don't you understand?" For an entire year, whenever someone walked through my door and announced, "Bill, you need to do this, you need to do that . . . ," I'd just point to the door and say, "See that sign? Read it. My fundamental calling is to be the pastor of a local church. If you're asking me if I am committed to building a biblically functioning community in South Barrington, Illinois, the answer is yes. Any other question—the answer is no."

In recent years I've felt called to try to help other churches. So my addendum calling is to serve the Willow Creek Association. But beyond that, my standard answer to most invitations is "No." I don't do executive dinners. I don't speak for corporations. I don't do men's retreats, marriage enrichment weekends, gospel cruises, or Holy Land trips.

I respectfully decline all but a fraction of the opportunities that come my way. As politely as I can, I explain to those making requests that what they are asking me to do is not in line with my primary calling. If I were to invest energy in what they're asking me to do I would have to take energy away from what God is asking me to do. And I am not willing to do that.

We leaders need to draw heavily on God's promise that if we remain focused and fulfill his calling, then he will empower us to endure. That's the kind of God we have. Second Chronicles 16:9 says, "The eyes of the Lord search all over the world (to do what?) to strongly support those whose hearts are fully his." To me this verse means that if leaders are fully obedient to the calling God has put on their lives, then he will strongly support them in fulfilling that calling.

In my darkest moments, when I was tempted to take the big dive, I always fell back on my firm belief that the assignment God had given me was sustainable—*if I was pursuing it right*. I've always been absolutely convinced that God knows what he's doing and he's not playing games with my life. So when my life felt unsustainable, I turned my attention to what I might be doing wrong. Of course there was always room for improvement.

Another reason I stopped short of leaving the ministry, even during the most difficult times, was that I never wanted to betray the One who gave me life, salvation, and the promise of eternity. The words of Paul have haunted me for almost thirty years. Fulfill your ministry. Don't bail. Don't quit. Figure out what you need to do to sustain your life in ministry, because quitting isn't an option.

Over the years hundreds of Christian leaders have asked me questions about calling: Am I in the right place? Do you think I'm doing the right thing? Did God wire me up for this? Do you think God is calling me to move into a new challenge? My standard answer is, "Why are you asking *me*? That's a Holy Spirit question. You have to do the same thing I have to do to get clarity on this calling stuff: Lay your heart open before the Holy Spirit and say, 'God lead my life. You are the potter, I am the clay. Show me the way. You speak and I'll listen.'"

Every leader must learn this kind of Holy Spirit dependence. If you do, God will make your calling sure. And being sure about your calling will provide the staying power you need.

SECOND COURSE: ENDURING BY DEVELOPING THE COURAGE TO CHANGE

THIS IS A 201 level course in the Graduate School of Endurance. It will stretch you and make you grow in ways you normally wouldn't choose. You'll also have to face parts of yourself you normally wouldn't face. The curriculum for this class is based on Paul's words in 1 Timothy 4:16, "Pay attention to yourself, and then to your teaching." Here's my paraphrase of this verse: "Examine yourself and examine your life. Then change whatever you can change that will lighten your load and help you prevail in your calling."

Sounds like common sense, doesn't it?

If you talk to leaders who are no longer in the game, a surprising number of them will sheepishly admit, "I should have taken more time off. I should have shared the preaching load. I should have developed teams to help me. I should have asked for a raise. I should have gotten more training. I should have modified my daily schedule. I should have found a mentor. I should have gotten into an accountability group. I should have had some Christian counseling. I should have taken up golf."

Stories of Those Who Didn't Change

I'll never forget the breakfast I once had with a famous pastor who had wound up in a moral ditch. My only agenda was to be a brother to him and to let him know that he still mattered to God.

That morning as we sat across from each other in the restaurant I asked, "How are you supporting your family?"

"Well," he shrugged, his voice full of sadness, "the family left, you know."

"Oh, I'm so sorry. I didn't know." I said quietly. "Then, how are you supporting yourself these days?"

He tried to form the words, but they kept getting stuck in his throat. Finally he sighed and said, "I'm selling shoes," after which he buried his face in his hands and began to sob.

No offense to anyone in retail sales, but this kingdom leader had not been called to sell footwear. For many years he had loved the challenge, the excitement, and the fulfillment of church leadership. But that morning at the breakfast table he knew he would never assume pastoral duties again. After he regained control of his emotions, he recounted a whole list of modifications he should have incorporated into his life that would likely have led to a totally different outcome. What made his pain even deeper that morning was knowing that he had considered making some of those changes years ago, but he hadn't done it.

When I ask leaders who have disqualified themselves from ministry why they didn't make changes that would have made their life more sustainable, the most frequent answer is, "I didn't have the guts. I couldn't muster the courage. I didn't want to ruffle anyone's feathers. I knew it would send the Nielsen ratings down. I was afraid people would think I wasn't committed or that I wasn't willing to suffer or sacrifice. I didn't want them thinking I wasn't a team player."

When I ask these same people what they would do differently if they had a do-over, I hear the same response every time: "I would examine my life and change whatever needed changing to increase the odds of sustainability. Then I would let the chips fall where they may. I probably would have displeased some people and taken some heat. But at least I'd still be in the ministry today."

To a person, these folks wish they had done things differently.

I don't know what your perception of me is. From a distance, I probably seem impervious to criticism. But I'm not. Actually I'm very sensitive to people's disapproval. I almost wrecked my life, my marriage, my ministry, and my health rather than risk peoples' displeasure with me. And I'll go so far as to tell you where my greatest point of sensitivity is: doing anything that will lead people to question my willingness to pay the price to be a committed follower of Christ.

The sensitivity regarding my perceived commitment level has made every sustainability decision excruciatingly painful for me.

Changing the Pace of My Life

Back in the early eighties no senior pastor I knew of was taking summer study breaks. There wasn't even language for that in the circles in which I ran. But I knew I needed a break. I remember going to the elders and explaining that the first seven years of Willow had taken a huge toll on me. We had grown from a handful of high school kids to several thousand people on a shoestring budget in rented facilities with a mostly volunteer staff. The accumulated hardships associated with that had left me emotionally drained and physically exhausted. The only way I could see myself getting healed up would be to find a hideaway several hours away from the church where I could take my family for a few weeks to regroup.

I was expecting instant support for my request for time off, but I didn't get it. I'll never forget the look of hesitation in the eyes of the elders. While they were genuinely concerned about me and my family, they also knew how crucial my leadership was during that era. We were in a multimillion dollar building program, money was tight, and the congregation was already feeling over-challenged. My absence could only make things worse. But the elders knew I was at my breaking point, so they had the wisdom (and grace) to grant me a three-week break.

After I informed the congregation of my plans for a break, I got a scathing letter from a man in the church: "Who do you think you are? You stand up in front of the congregation and challenge us to sacrifice, serve, and give—and then you run off to the nearest beach. Are you the exception to the commitment rule? I've been with my company for fifteen years, and do you know how many vacation days I get a year? Ten. That's all! You're a wet-behind-the-ears pastor and you're going to take a three-week summer vacation? Give me a break!" And on and on it went.

I was devastated. I leaned back in my squeaky, third-hand office chair and felt nauseated.

I began flirting with the idea of canceling my badly needed break. Carnal macho pride welled up in me to the point that I thought about intentionally working myself to death. *I'll show you!* I thought. *You want to see commitment? I'll preach myself into the grave or the nuthouse ... whatever comes first. That will prove, once and for all, who around here is really committed!*

But hours later, healthier inclinations prevailed. I tore up his letter and went home to help the family pack for my study break.

Without being melodramatic, that three-week vacation probably saved my family and my ministry. It paved the way for an annual study break with my wife and kids that has sustained us for over twenty years. I can honestly say that I would not have lasted in pastoral ministry without those summer breaks. Nor would my family. But summoning up the courage to go on that first break was one of the hardest things I've ever done.

Incidentally, a few weeks after I returned from that inaugural study break, the guy who had written me that letter (I still think of him as the Willow Unabomber) came down to the bullpen to talk to me. He said, "Do you remember that mean letter I wrote you? I was in a terrible mood that day. I needed to blow off some steam. I hope you didn't take it seriously. And I hope that you had a wonderful vacation."

Driving home from church that day I thought to myself, *I almost wrecked my life over a single letter from a guy who didn't even mean what he wrote. Scary!*

Years later I had dinner with a former pastor and internationally known author whose moral choices had disqualified him from ministry. His story almost paralleled mine, except that the person who told him not to take a break was a deacon in his church. When the time-off this leader requested was denied, he clicked into that competitive I'll-show-you-how-committed-I-can-be gear that I had toyed with and he kept up the soul-shattering pace. He eventually preached himself into the kind of exhaustion that makes moral collapse almost inevitable.

What a tragedy for the whole kingdom.

But that story didn't have to turn out that way. Yes, it takes great courage to make the tough decisions that increase ministerial sustainability. But we can—and must—make those decisions.

Changing How You Do Ministry

I reached another breaking point in the early nineties. The preaching load at Willow was starting to wear me down. I was teaching at two midweek services and four weekend services, not to mention holiday services, staff meetings, leadership retreats, and church leaders' conferences. Almost every waking moment of my day was spent studying for messages, writing messages, praying for messages, delivering messages, and recuperating from giving messages. I began to think of myself as a message machine. I'd joke with my kids, "I need some illustrations. Go do something message-worthy. Get kicked out of school—whatever it takes. I just need material!"

But eventually I realized the message mill that was taking a toll on me was no longer a joking matter. It was draining me emotionally and spiritually. I began to dread the very thought of another teaching assignment. I fantasized about going back into the marketplace and even entertained a few offers from business friends before I realized what was driving all of this: Too much teaching.

God had not changed my calling. I still had enormous passion for the local church. I was still convinced it was the hope of the world. I just couldn't bear the thought that every day for the rest of my life I was going to be three days—at the most!—away from having to give a brand new message.

So one day I decided to get on the solution side of the issue and I prayed to God for creativity. Within hours I had sketched out a proposal around the concept of team teaching. The idea was that I would raise up a team of men and women with the spiritual gift of teaching. Then I would coach them to the point where the people at Willow wouldn't care who was teaching at any given service. I would lead the team, make the teaching assignments, and still do a portion of the teaching. But sharing the load was the only way I felt I could stay in ministry.

I ran my idea by some of my pastor- and church-consultant friends. To my utter dismay, almost everybody hated the idea. "It'll never work. Churches need one communicator, especially large churches," they warned. Others said, "Only the senior pastor should have the pulpit. Sharing it will invite disaster." I received negative feedback from every recognized church authority with whom I talked. When our elders discussed the concept they were very disheartened to hear the opinions of the experts. But they were also sobered by the knowledge that I was sinking fast and we had no other options on the table. So we pleaded for help from God and moved ahead.

As we formed a teaching team and began sharing the load, the response was predictable: "I've only heard Bill for fifteen years. I don't want to hear anyone else. Who is the new guy? Why is he up there while Bill is sitting in the front row?" The inevitable comparisons were made and attendance even dropped when certain teachers did multiweek series, but we kept at it, continuing to coach the new teachers and praying that God would mature our congregation.

A decade later, we have no regrets about team teaching. Our people have not only accepted it but embraced it. I doubt that anyone at Willow would ever wish to go back to the days of a solo communicator.

The point, again, is that sustainability requires intentional, solution-side thinking and the courage to stick with a new approach even when you encounter resistance. Often the price seems high, but in the end it is worth it.

Making Difficult Personal Changes

One of the hardest changes I ever had to make was a very personal change. This change was about me more than it was about the church. It was an inner-world adjustment. Some of my friends had been encouraging me to see a professional Christian counselor, but I had resisted. Certainly my pride caused some hesitation, but beyond that I was concerned about the reputation of my family and the church. I worried that people might not understand my reasons for seeking help.

But finally I decided to go, and sure enough, within weeks of my first appointment, my office started receiving calls from across the country and from around the world, "Is it true that Bill Hybels is having an emotional breakdown?" My assistant would respond, "Well, he's seeing a Christian counselor for some personal development issues." "Oh," they'd say, "we heard he'd cracked up!" Or, "We heard that his marriage was going down."

Hearing these rumors added to the already difficult challenge of sitting in the waiting room of a Christian therapist's office. But there was a lot at risk. I knew there was no way I could continue to lead, teach, feed, and grow our church with so many broken pieces rattling around inside me. I had to take the time to reassemble my inner world if I wanted to stay in ministry. As difficult as this era was, without the insights I received and the healing I experienced through counseling I would not have been able to move into the joy-filled ministry I experienced through the rest of the nineties and into the new millennium.

The point I'm highlighting again is that every significant change I've made to ensure a sustainable life in ministry has been awkward, difficult, and painful. The risk of receiving people's disapproval and of damaging the church were very real and very frightening. More than once, I felt like I was betting the farm for the sake of my own health.

Let me mention one more example of a risk-reward dilemma. After months of appointments, my counselor suggested that I reflect on all the forms of recreation I was involved in and determine which one was the most restorative and why.

I said, "That doesn't require reflection. That's easy. I don't do anything for recreation."

After getting over his shock my counselor simply said, "Bill, you'd better start. Immediately."

That's when I began thinking about sailing again. As a kid I had raced small sailboats with my dad. During my teen years I had spent my summers in a tiny harbor town on Lake Michigan where I learned to sail the *Ann Gail,* a forty-five-foot yawl my dad had purchased in Ireland and sailed across the ocean. Sailing was, by far, the most replenishing recreation I had ever engaged in. But I gave it up abruptly when my father died of a heart attack and the *Ann Gail* was sold.

After several weeks of listening to me share both my love for sailing and my reluctance to pick it up again, my counselor gently pulled out of me the truth about why I was so worried about returning to sailing. What came out of my mouth surprised even me. "If I were to buy a sailboat, some magazine would take pictures of it that made it look twice as big. They'd call it a yacht and turn it into a big scandal, and then Willow and church leaders everywhere would have to deal with it, so . . . forget it! My sailing days are over."

He shook his head and said, "Sounds to me like you're making a fear-based decision. It's true, some people might disagree with a pastor having a boat. And yes, there's even the possibility of distorted media reports. But if you're really so worried about other people's perceptions, consider how it will look when you're in an institution weaving potholders at age forty.

"Bill," he said, "you need to schedule life-giving recreation on a regular basis if you intend to stay healthy over the long haul. God made you that way. I suggest that you move from the fear side of this equation to the faith side and start looking at boats!"

Many months later Lynne and I purchased a used, banged-up, thirty-five-foot race boat that brought more joy into my life than I could ever have imagined. Over the years whenever I took Willow people sailing, we'd drive up to the boat and I'd point to it and say, "See that hunk of fiberglass. That saved my ministry!" And in some ways it did.

Often when I'm out alone on a boat I can feel the smile of God coming my way. I can sense his saying, "Bill, you're more than a ministry machine to me. You're my son. I built you with a love for the wind, the water, and the motion of the waves. When you're on a boat, smiling and loving your life, I smile too—all across heaven."

In retrospect, I shudder to think where I'd be today had I not given myself permission to take up boating again.

As I enter my sixth decade of life with nearly thirty years of ministry behind me, my life feels more sustainable than at any other time—ever. From where I stand, my future seems bright. My marriage and family relationships bring me great joy. My energy for ministry and living is increasing. My passion for the capital-C church worldwide is growing. My love for God, for worship, and for lost people is escalating by the year.

This is a life I can sustain and love. This is also the kind of life I yearn for every church leader to experience. In John 10:10, Jesus referred to this kind of life as "life in all its fullness." How I long for the day when pastors and church leaders will not just preach this passage to others but will make the difficult life-management decisions that will enable this passage to become descriptive of their own daily experience.

How Do You Handle the Things You Can't Change?

Whenever I encourage leaders to change whatever they can to make life more sustainable, I know there are also some things they can't change. What then? I know pastors whose calling has led them to build churches in poverty-stricken or racially charged or war-torn areas. The circumstances surrounding their lives will probably take generations to change. What then? I know other church leaders whose denominations resist any change and give their clergy marching orders that are rigid and outdated. What then?

The apostle Paul had a troublesome condition in his life that he referred to as a "thorn." He prayed to God to remove it, but apparently it never went away. The more I get to know other Christian leaders, the more I'm convinced that almost all of us have at least one troubling circumstance that we cannot seem to change—a thorn that forces us to turn to God daily and say, "Darn it, God. It hurts again today. For the life of me I don't understand why you don't remove this. But there's a reason why you are God and I am me. So I'll trust you through another day."

How do you handle a thorn? You talk to God about it. You express your frustration. You scream and cry, if you must. But eventually you claim God's words to Paul, "My grace is sufficient for you" (2 Corinthians 12:9).

Another way to handle a thorn is to refuse to look at the rest of your life in one linear timeline. Instead you break your life into bite-sized chunks and pray, "God, all I need to do is trust in your sustaining power for one more twenty-four period. Help me endure this thorn until the sun goes down . . . we'll handle tomorrow, tomorrow."

This approach works, friends. I've practiced it for years. It builds faith and character. It contributes to radical reliance on God (which is a good thing). And it increases our confidence that we have the capacity to endure over the long haul.

THIRD COURSE: ENDURING BY DISCOVERING SAFE PEOPLE

THE NEXT CLASS IS a 301 level course in the Graduate School of Endurance, and quite frankly, it's a part of the curriculum that most Christian leaders never get around to taking.

This class is based on Galatians 6:2, "Bear each other's burdens and so fulfill the law of Christ." When I meet leaders who have led passionately for a long time, they can usually tell me (in graphic detail) of the time when they made the transition from being self-sufficient, independent types to becoming people who lean deeply into community. They usually describe a breaking point when their frustration came to an all-time high and their despair was at an all-time low. But just when they were on the brink of taking the big dive they decided to say a simple four-letter word: Help. They said to someone they trusted, "Please help me. This one's a heart-wrecker. I can't handle this alone. Someone has to help me bear this burden."

Even Jesus, the most resilient leader who ever lived, said to a small group of friends, "My soul is deeply grieved to the point of death. Would some of you please stay with me? Would you be with me? Would you help me?" (Matthew 26:38, my paraphrase).

Jesus was freely admitting his need for safe people. Eventually all of us leaders will have to do the same. Sustainability demands it.

I'm the first one to admit that church work confuses relational worlds more than any other profession. As Christians, we're all supposed to love each other, be brothers and sisters to each other, pray for each other, and generally support and watch out for each other. But get a church leader off to the side and ask the questions, "Do you really have a safe person you can turn to in trying times? Do you have someone to whom you could admit your thoughts about bailing out of ministry? Is there anybody to whom you could confess the escapist sins that are becoming very tantalizing to you again? Is there anybody you trust enough to tell them *anything?*"

Ask a hundred Christian leaders those questions and an alarmingly high percentage will stare at their shoes and say, "No." They may say they have prayer partners or they periodically participate in a small group, but very few church leaders can even imagine relating to a few friends in a deeply intimate way.

This causes me great concern. I don't want to be a prophet of doom, but I am afraid that a steady stream of church leaders are going to disappear—tragically—from the rosters of kingdom leadership unless they commit themselves to discovering safe people and leaning into those relationships. Our hearts were not built to handle the hardships and heartbreaks of ministry alone. We need to link up with a few folks who can help us bear the heavy burdens of our lives.

Recently I learned of yet another high-profile Christian leader who was permanently sidelined because of moral failure. I was with him just before his problem became public. I didn't know what he was facing, but I sensed there was trouble in his life. I asked a few semi-probing questions to see if he would open up to me, but I could tell he wasn't ready for that. I carefully inquired about his willingness to see a Christian counselor. He was incredulous that I would suggest something so dramatic.

"I'm fine, it's nothing," he said, closing the door to further discussion.

When I received word of his fall, I shook my head and let loose an expletive that I had to confess later on. How many more leaders will we lose before we acknowledge our need to lean into safe relationships?

I have learned over the years that I am not strong enough to face the rigors of church work alone. In addition to the support of my wife and kids, I need the support of close friends. I need a small circle of trusted brothers and sisters with whom I can discuss temptations lest I fall to them. I need a few safe people with whom I can process feelings of frustration so that I don't become emotionally toxic. I need a few people in my life who will reflect grace back to me when I have fouled up and feel unusable.

It's a powerful thing to receive grace from fellow human beings. I learned how to accept God's grace many years ago, and I could not have survived ministry—or life, for that matter—without it. But seeing acceptance in the eyes of grace-giving people to whom I have confessed an ugly sin is an equally unforgettable experience. Every leader needs it.

So let me throw out the challenge one more time: Leaders, please find safe people. It might take you years—that's how long it took me—but don't get discouraged in the search. Keep praying and looking and trusting God to provide. It might make all the difference in whether or not you endure.

THE FINAL CLASS: ENDURING WITH AN ETERNAL PERSPECTIVE

I GUARANTEE THAT THIS class in the Graduate School of Endurance will not be easy. It's called "Learning How to Live with an Eternal Perspective," and it has to do with the nature of time.

Let me illustrate: Every summer my sailing crew and I have to deliver my sailboat by water to various harbors around the Great Lakes for regattas. If you're not from the Midwest you probably don't realize how large Lake Michigan is. It's approximately a hundred miles across and over three hundred miles from north to south.

A hundred-mile delivery at six or seven knots on a sailboat translates into a twelve-hour cruise. Occasionally I draw the short straw and wind up with delivery duty. More than once I have gotten a quarter of the way across Lake Michigan only to run smack into lightning, thunderstorms, and huge winds. Usually I do deliveries alone, which is what I prefer, but it does raise the ante when the weather turns ugly. On more than one occasion I've encountered conditions that made me wonder if I was going to make it to the other side.

Those moments are very intense. Sooner or later, though, I gather my wits about me and remind myself of another perspective on Lake Michigan. It's a perspective with which I'm very familiar, a pilot's perspective. I earned my pilot's license when I was a teenager and I've flown across Lake Michigan in private planes hundreds of times.

A flight across Lake Michigan in a pilot's seat offers an entirely different perspective of the lake. Distances are compressed and threats are minimized. A hundred miles of visibility is common in an airplane, so with enough altitude, you can easily see all the way across the lake. Waves that may be pounding the hull of a boat violently look small and tame from the air. A fast plane can transport you from one side of Lake Michigan to the other in just a matter of minutes. In fact, pilots of corporate jets often refer to crossing Lake Michigan as "skipping over the pond."

So when I'm delivering a boat across Lake Michigan and find myself in ugly conditions, I try to bring the pilot's perspective to my sailing situation. In my mind I look down at my plight from the cockpit of a private jet cruising at 25,000 feet. I imagine the higher view and say to myself, *From up here the other coastline is already visible. From up here the harbor is in clear view. From up here the waves appear very manageable.*

Believe it or not, with that viewpoint in mind I can hang in there. I can keep going. I can begin to believe that I'm actually going to make it, providing I persevere. But I need that other perspective to give me hope and renewed determination. You know where I'm going with this.

Heroic Christian leaders throughout redemptive history have always looked at the difficulty of their short-term struggles against the backdrop of eternity. The apostle Paul said in 2 Corinthians

4:17, "For the light, momentary afflictions that we bear are producing in us an eternal weight of glory far beyond all comparison." In this passage Paul is suggesting that when the difficulties of life appear overwhelming we need to think more like pilots than like sailors. We need to look at the waves from *above* them rather than *in* them. That is what it means to look at life from an eternal perspective.

And by the way, what were the "light, momentary afflictions" that Paul had to look at from a pilot's perspective? In the previous verses he lists them, "I've been afflicted, confused, persecuted, constantly hunted down, threatened to be killed for the cause of Christ." But he says, "I will not lose heart" (2 Corinthians 4:8, 16).

How could Paul possibly endure those trials? Is he made of better stuff than you or me? Not necessarily. The apostle Paul endured because he had learned how to live with an eternal perspective. He had learned how to look at present hardships from a broader viewpoint that reminded him that the harbor was not that far away.

Like Paul, we can endure if we have the right perspective.

Over twenty years ago I adopted as my life verse these words penned by the apostle Paul, "Be steadfast, immovable, always abounding in the work of the Lord, knowing that your labor is not in vain if it is in the Lord" (1 Corinthians 15:58). Paraphrased: No matter how difficult the hardship, no matter how long a particular storm lasts, no matter how dark and scary it gets, no matter how the winds howl and the waves crash . . . choose the path of courage. Be steadfast. Be immovable. Endure.

Essentially Paul is saying, "Decide in advance that you are never going to quit. Decide in advance that you are going to keep abounding in the work of the Lord no matter how high the pain level rises. Decide in advance that you are going to keep showing up, trusting, serving, proclaiming the gospel, discipling, shepherding, leading, and casting the vision." That's courageous leadership.

What's the payoff? Knowing that "your work is not in vain, if it is in the Lord."

From an eternal perspective, the harbor, the commendation of God, and heaven are not all that far away!

Someday we are going to stand face to face with the Son of God who never gave up on his redemptive calling. We're going to stand face to face with a finisher who didn't quit when his teachings were criticized. Who didn't quit when his trusted followers deserted him. Who didn't quit when he was mocked, beaten, and spit upon. Who didn't quit when the nails were driven through his hands and his feet. Who didn't quit as his atoning blood splashed from his veins to the dust beneath the cross.

Only when Jesus' ministry had been completely fulfilled, when his race had been completely run, did he say those final words. And he said them with high octane, "It is finished. My job is done now. I did what my Father asked me to do. I hung in there all the way to the end and I fulfilled my ministry."

When we meet Christ personally, I think we will all be prompted to say, "Jesus Christ, thanks for fulfilling your ministry. Thanks for not bailing out on the way to the cross. Because you endured, you purchased my pardon, you transformed my life, you protected my family, you sustained my church, you changed my world, and you sealed my eternal destiny."

Hopefully all of us leaders will also be able to add, "And Jesus, because of your example and with your help, I finished my ministry too."

How we're going to revel in those moments! How glad we will be that we didn't quit.

STAYING THE COURSE

A FEW MONTHS AGO a cruel disease took the life of one of my closest friends. This book is dedicated to him. As I write these words I am fighting to hold back a river of tears. Jon Rasmussen was a brother, a mentor, a sailing partner, a fellow soldier, a servant, a confidante, and truly one of the most remarkable men I've ever known.

Two days before his death I knelt by his bedside and told him one last time that I loved him with all my heart and that I would see him on the other side. With labored motion he reached for a present that he had arranged for me. Opening the carefully wrapped box, I discovered a beautiful silver mariner's compass. Before I could protest his thoughtfulness and generosity, Jon whispered, "Bill, your life gave my life direction. From the day we met, God used you to show me how my life could have purpose and meaning, and I can't thank you enough.

"Read the backside," he whispered. I read the three words engraved on the silver surface with tears in my eyes: "Stay the course." After reading those words I climbed onto the bed and embraced Jon for several moments, then prayed for him.

Two days later Jon died. Doing his funeral was one of the hardest things I've ever done. But I will treasure his final gift to me like few other earthly possessions I own.

Stay the course. Stay the course. Stay the course.

If I do—if all of us leaders do—we will win the day for the glory of the One whose name we bear.

Rediscovering Church

*The Story and Vision of
Willow Creek Community Church*

Lynne and Bill Hybels

Rediscovering Church is the candid story of Willow Creek Community Church's phenomenal growth, from 100 members meeting in a Palatine, Illinois, movie theater to its present Sunday morning attendance of 15,000. Bill Hybels and his wife, Lynne, tell about Willow Creek's beginnings, its struggles, the philosophy behind its success, and the strategies that have made it a model for church growth.

The first half of the book, written by Lynne Hybels, explores the early years of Willow Creek and the personal accounts behind one of this century's most remarkable church stories. It offers an honest look at the ways God has used both the strengths and weaknesses of His people, creating a church of believers who have had tremendous impact for Christ in their community.

In the second half of *Rediscovering Church,* Bill Hybels helps you apply the strengths of Willow Creek's ministry philosophy to your own congregation's mission. From mission statements to developing leadership, making sound financial decisions, and handling growth, Bill stresses that God wants to build His church to be an effective and committed community of faith that reaches out to a hurting world, to be the body of Christ in real and tangible ways.

Rediscovering Church draws on the experiences of Willow Creek to show how one fellowship crystallized its mission and methodology, its vision and values. The Willow Creek story provides an example that churches and individuals alike can turn to for inspiration, encouragement, and a means of uncovering the pattern for their own unique mission and ministry.

Softcover: 0-310-21927-2

Pick up a copy at your favorite bookstore!

ZONDERVAN™

GRAND RAPIDS, MICHIGAN 49530 USA

WWW.ZONDERVAN.COM